What if the most difficult elements our confusion, our times of spiritua actually hold the most promise? In highly readable language, Andrew Arndt combs Scripture, historical Christian witness, his own experience, and three striking contemporary examples to make a compelling case for the redemptive power of suffering. I read *All Flame* in one mesmerized sitting and finished with a sense that something had shifted within me. *All Flame* is an important book. Read, and be changed.

> CAROLYN ARENDS, *recording artist; author;*
> *Renovaré director of education*

All Flame may very well be the invitation into intimacy with God your soul has been longing to receive. So many guides to Christian spirituality unwittingly distance the one they are seeking to introduce—through inaccessible mysticism, unattainable pietism, or uninspiring intellectualism—but *All Flame* celebrates the wonderful proximity of God for every single one of us. I particularly appreciate its Trinitarian approach, its rich biographical examples, and above all— its grace.

> PETE GREIG, *founder of 24-7 Prayer*

Andrew Arndt has unearthed a tremendous amount of truth and revelation in this timely book. Andrew is serious but fun and scholarly but approachable in these pages. His words are sharp, penetrating, and much needed. You will follow Jesus better after reading this.

> BRADY BOYD, *senior pastor of New Life Church;*
> *author of* Extravagant

Herein lies the passion of a contemplative—one who is devoted to the mysterious relationship of God and humanity. This book will inspire you to deepen your faith and give you courage to travel with the Holy Spirit where you've dared not venture before.

PHILEENA HEUERTZ, *founding partner of Gravity, a Center for Contemplative Activism; author of* Pilgrimage of a Soul *and* Mindful Silence

The ongoing project of spiritual formation requires an intentional integration with the mystery of the triune God. The very nature of God points to the ways we need to be formed. Yet this kind of integration can be difficult for many to present. Enter Andrew Arndt. Andrew is a pastor and thinker who has an uncanny ability to make complicated things accessible. This book is textured and nuanced, and it will provide you with a beautiful framework to become all flame. I highly recommend it.

RICH VILLODAS, *lead pastor of New Life Fellowship*

Andrew Arndt's pastoral heart burns through these pages, bringing to light the goodness of resting in the presence of Father, Son, and Spirit. At a time when Christians are often exhorted to find their identity "in Christ alone," Andrew reminds us to appreciate the vital ministry of each person of the triune God. And he calls us into the grace of the dying life, into the self-surrender that is a hallmark of every season lived within God's Kingdom. Wise, gentle, and incisive, Andrew navigates the spiritual terrain with an awareness that even in the darkness, even when we feel forsaken, there is still flame, nourishing a longing to be united to that holy presence.

TINA BOESCH, *author of* Given

Andrew writes from a depth of biblical and personal experience, mining the riches buried within the joys and sorrows of life, bringing forth the burning glory of a life set fire by the Father, Son, and Holy Spirit.

GEOFF HOLSCLAW, *professor; pastor; coauthor of* Does God Really Like Me?

With *All Flame*, Andrew has written my very favorite sort of book: telling stories to explore ideas we often consider too complex and inaccessible. Andrew explores Bible stories, Kingdom stories, and real-life stories, and the Father, Son, and Holy Spirit seem close enough to touch. Read this book, find yourself in these stories, and encounter the flame of God's presence right here.

CATHERINE McNIEL, *author of* Long Days of Small Things *and* All Shall Be Well

How do we know God and become known by God? *All Flame* invites us into the wild mystery of the triune God with conversational charm and disarming simplicity.

GLENN PACKIAM, *author of* Blessed, Broken, Given

We may have discovered a worthy successor to the late Eugene Peterson. Without any condescension, we are invited to join Andrew on a journey into the love, holiness, and unity of the Trinity and the paradoxical power of being a devoted follower of Jesus.

CHARLIE SELF, *visiting professor of church history at* Assemblies of God Theological Seminary

The most important thing in life, said Dallas Willard, is to develop deep friendship with the Holy Trinity. This book by Andrew Arndt serves as the perfect guide into the depths. There's no doubt in my mind that *All Flame* will serve as a sort of burning-bush experience for many.

DANIEL GROTHE, *author of* Chasing Wisdom

Pastors whose lives exude the love of God are far rarer than they should be. Andrew Arndt is one such pastor, and when you read *All Flame*, you'll understand why. This book will make you think, but more importantly, it will expand your soul.

JR ROZKO, *national director of Missio Alliance*

This book is like a brand-new song we've always known. Andrew so eloquently writes us into passion. A burning for union with God so true that it lights up everything. This is the sound of something holy, and I plan to listen on repeat.

JON EGAN, *worship leader at New Life Church*

In *All Flame*, Andrew Arndt exquisitely blends the Scriptures, the Church's great thinkers, and his own personal and pastoral experience into a candid and compelling look at the Christian life.

JASON R. JACKSON, *associate lead pastor at New Life Downtown*

This book begins with the story of a liar who stole his brother's life and ends with the story of a saint whose life was stolen from him. In those stories, and in what lies between them, Arndt reminds us, sometimes gently, sometimes not, that God is holy and we are not—*yet*. This is a book that won't let us forget that in spite of the fact we are more like the liar than the saint, there's still a promise in the threat of the gospel: God is nearer than our pain, even if sometimes that nearness is itself painful.

CHRIS GREEN, *pastor at The Summit Church*

Arndt delivers at every level, calling Christians to reconsider the life-altering reality of the Triune God and his gospel. With creativity and clarity, Arndt challenges us to awaken to God, fear not the trials, and arrive at Christlike holiness.

BENJAMIN QUINN, *assistant professor of theology and history of ideas at Southeastern Baptist Theological Seminary*

Andrew Arndt plunges us into the mystery of the triune God and shows how the flames of heaven heal the wounds of humanity and vanquish the gates of hell.

BRETT DAVIS, *teaching pastor at New Life Church*

ALL FLAME

Entering into the Life of the Father, Son, and Holy Spirit

ANDREW ARNDT

A NavPress resource published in alliance
with Tyndale House Publishers

NavPress is the publishing ministry of The Navigators, an international Christian organization and leader in personal spiritual development. NavPress is committed to helping people grow spiritually and enjoy lives of meaning and hope through personal and group resources that are biblically rooted, culturally relevant, and highly practical.

For more information, visit NavPress.com.

For Mandi,
and our four kids:
Ethan, Gabe,
Bella, and Liam.

I can't believe God gave us to one another.

Thanks be to God for this indescribable gift.

CONTENTS

INTRODUCTION

Surely the LORD is in this place,
and I was not aware of it.
GENESIS 28:16

If you will, you can become all flame.
ABBA JOSEPH TO ABBA LOT

Hi. My name is Andrew. I've been a pastor since 2006 and a follower of Jesus all my life.

I want to say some things to you about God. And about being human. And about the intersection of those two things.

What happens when God and the human life get tangled up with one another? What does it look like? What does it feel like? When we decide to yield our lives to the God whose character we see in the person of Jesus, what should we expect? What does it do to us? What are the core movements of the spiritual life?

The truth is, "God and the human life getting tangled up with one another" is as urgent a reality now as it has ever been. The apostle Paul many centuries ago wrote that "the creation waits in eager expectation for the children of God to be revealed."[1] In Paul's vision of reality, the redemption of humanity in the holy love of God and the healing of the cosmos were vitally bound up with one another.

Our time is desperate for the sons and daughters of the living God to be revealed. They are called sons and daughters because their lives have come to reflect the character of the God who is all holy love, and as such, they represent an ongoing and deliberate advance against the darkness of our world. They are peacemakers, reconcilers, sages. They are men and women of God who, having given themselves over to the ecstatic and agonizing process of spiritual transformation, are able to bring liberation, blessing, and healing to a world grown weary with sin.

I believe that Paul's dream resonates with us because it was and is God's dream *first*. The trouble is, most of us never get there. We bail out on the process of transformation—by which our lives come to represent the character of God—before he is through with us.

This is a tragedy of the first order, and it has to do— I believe—with our expectations. While creation waits in eager *expectation* for the children of God to be revealed, many of us simply *expect* to be able to pray a prayer or sign a statement of faith and have everything turn out hunky-dory. We have little concept of faith as a journey, a story, a sometimes-gut-wrenching process by which holiness is formed in us. And so, when *crises* in the journey of faith hit, we think that something is malfunctioning. Overwhelmed by disillusionment, we opt out of the long, beautiful, and often-painful process of spiritual transformation, and the children of God remain veiled to the world's eyes.

This is as ruinous as it is unnecessary. God has so much

more for all of us. Through all of life's ups and downs, triumphs and tragedies, mountaintop experiences and places of gnawing loneliness, he can and will make us sons and daughters—living, breathing, walking images-in-miniature of his own glory and goodness—if we'll let him. We will find our fullness in him, and the world will be healed.

That, in a nutshell, is what this book is about.

BECOMING AWARE

There's a fabulous story about a man named Jacob told in the Old Testament. He's fleeing from his family, having cheated his twin brother, Esau (the firstborn), out of the birthright *and* their father Isaac's blessing. And now, at his father's bidding, Jacob is headed to a place called Haran[2] to try to find a wife for himself. It's a big moment for the young man—a cocktail of tension and hope and heartache, spiked with terror and possibility.

I'm sure you've been there. I have too. Moments when you feel great tectonic forces beneath your feet causing the ground of your once comfortable and predictable life to buckle and quake, and you know that whatever the outcome, things will never be the same. There will be no going back to how things were. And so—because there is no other option—you put it all on the line, holding on for dear life.

That's what was going on with Jacob when we catch up with him somewhere outside Haran. He's been traveling all day and decides to stop to sleep for a while. Using a stone for a pillow, the physically and emotionally exhausted Jacob falls into a deep sleep. The writer of Genesis tells us what happened during Jacob's slumber:

He had a dream in which he saw a stairway resting on the earth, with its top reaching to heaven, and the angels of God were ascending and descending on it. There above it stood the LORD, and he said: "I am the LORD, the God of your father Abraham and the God of Isaac. I will give you and your descendants the land on which you are lying. Your descendants will be like the dust of the earth, and you will spread out to the west and to the east, to the north and to the south. All peoples on earth will be blessed through you and your offspring. I am with you and will watch over you wherever you go, and I will bring you back to this land. I will not leave you until I have done what I have promised you." [3]

God appears to Jacob. In the midst of Jacob's questions and concerns, in the midst of his stress and heartache over the rupture in his relationship with his brother, in the midst of his hopes and dreams . . . *God appears to Jacob*, both as the exalted, transcendent, sovereign God (which is what the writer is saying by situating God above the stairway) and also as the everywhere-present one,[4] affirming to Jacob that no matter the circumstance or appearance, "I am *with you* and will watch over you *wherever you go*" and "*I will not leave you*."

I'm a big dreamer. For me, most nights are jam-packed with dreams. I don't *often*, however, have dreams like this. Dreams of angels ascending and descending and a ladder stretching from earth to heaven and the Lord of all creation making solemn vows to me . . .

Apparently, Jacob didn't either.

The magnitude of it shook him out of his slumber, and he

remarked to himself, "Surely the LORD is in this place, and I was not aware of it."[5] And at that very moment of awareness, terror overtakes him. The Scripture says that "[Jacob] was afraid and said, 'How awesome is this place! This is none other than the house of God; this is the gate of heaven.'"[6]

I love that line. "Surely the LORD is in this place," Jacob muses, *"and I was not aware of it."* Isn't that, more or less, the story with most of us, most of the time?

A DEEPER KIND OF "KNOWING"

To add a little depth to the picture, it is interesting to observe that the Hebrew word that the writer of Genesis puts on Jacob's lips for "aware" is the word *yada`*. Generally speaking, *yada`* is translated "know." As in "Surely the LORD is in this place, and I did not *know* it." It wasn't until Jacob fell into the depths of his dream-filled slumber that he finally "woke up" to the all-encompassing presence of God, making promises, willing a bright future for him.

So far, so good.

But there's more still. When *we* today hear the word *know*, we generally think of *information*. I "know" my Social Security number. You "know" your parents' birthdays (maybe). We "know" that Columbus sailed the ocean blue in fourteen hundred and ninety-two. That sort of thing. *Information.*

But for the ancient Hebrews, *yada`*, while including what we might call *information*, went way beyond it. Here's a good example of the deep meaning of the word *yada`*, from earlier in Genesis: "Now Adam *yada`* Eve his wife, and she conceived."[7]

Ahem.

Clearly, *yada`* is more than mere "information." *Yada`* is deep, experiential knowledge of the other. Adam did not "know" in some kind of detached, academic way that Eve was five feet, six inches tall with brown hair, blue-green eyes, a nice smile, an easy laugh, and a winning personality (I might have just described my wife there). . . . This is about, well, the kind of (what theologians would call) "comingling" of personhood where the "knower" knows-and-is-known in the deepest, most intimate ways possible. It's an up-close-and-personal, highly relational kind of knowing. It is a knowing that, to put it mildly, is *productive*. It is *fruitful*. Adam and Eve "knew" each other, and Cain came forth. We *know* the Lord, and our lives become fruitful.

That "knowing" of God's encompassing presence is what Jacob says he *did not have* until his fast-asleep vision of God pulled the blinders back from his eyes. From that point on, wherever he went and whatever he did, Jacob would live his life with an intimate, experiential knowledge that in all things and at all times, *it was God with whom he dealt*. And he would be fruitful as a result.

WRESTLING WITH GOD

Years later, the paths of the estranged brothers Jacob and Esau would cross. Jacob was riddled with anxiety. Sending a caravan ahead of him, he remained behind, and once more, Jacob meets God, in a scene that has captivated the imaginations of skeptic and believer alike for generations:

Jacob was left alone, and a man wrestled with him till daybreak. When the man saw that he could not overpower him, he touched the socket of Jacob's hip so that his hip was wrenched as he wrestled with the man. Then the man said, "Let me go, for it is daybreak."

But Jacob replied, "I will not let you go unless you bless me."

The man asked him, "What is your name?"

"Jacob," he answered.

Then the man said, "Your name will no longer be Jacob, but Israel, because you have struggled with God and with humans and have overcome."

Jacob said, "Please tell me your name."

But he replied, "Why do you ask my name?" Then he blessed him there.

So Jacob called the place Peniel, saying, "It is because I saw God face to face, and yet my life was spared." [8]

Jacob, rife with anxiety over the meeting with Esau, wrestling internally with the imminent encounter with his now very powerful big brother, in fact wrestles with God. And in the encounter, he is changed. No longer is his name Jacob (the name means something like "deceiver"—a kind of permanent black mark on his character). Now his name is Israel, which means something like "he wrestles" or "he struggles." The man—God, as it turns out—says as much to him: "You have struggled with God and with humans and have overcome."

Jacob recognizes that he has encountered the infinite God in the finite struggle and calls the place Peniel—which means "face of God"—saying, "It is because I saw God face to face, and yet my life was spared." Hear this:

In all things,
at all times,
it is God with whom you deal.

The sooner we come to grips with this, the sooner we "know" the face of God in, with, and under the circumstances of our lives to shape us for his glory and draw us to himself, the better. When we engage honestly and fearlessly with God in the stuff and substance of our lives, we are changed. We become who God means us to be—creatures radiant with his own life and holiness.

On the other hand, when we shrink back from that knowing, when we deliberately act as though God does not exist or that our choices one way or another do not really matter, when we fail to wake up to his presence at all and instead live in denial or (worse) spend our lives blaming our circumstances and situations, we become shadowy, opaque, unreal. We diminish.

I don't want to diminish.

I know you don't, either.

BECOMING ALL FLAME

I want to grow in what the ancient men and women of faith often called "union with God"—that state of being where God is so present to and alive in us that it is difficult to know where God ends and we begin. Where by grace we grow into "God-likeness." Where we become like the burning bush of Exodus 3—on fire with glory, but not consumed. *Burning but not burned up . . .*

"Glory" was one of the apostle Paul's characteristic ways of talking about this state of being. Addressing a group of believers in the ancient city of Corinth, he wrote,

> We all, who with unveiled faces contemplate the Lord's glory, are being transformed into his image with ever-increasing glory, which comes from the Lord, who is the Spirit.[9]

I love that. Paul is saying that as we face the living God, something profound happens to us—we are transformed into his image, his likeness, with glory that always increases and never stops. Ever. We keep changing and expanding both to *look more like God* and to *contain and display more of his glory.*

There's a story told in *The Sayings of the Desert Fathers* that illustrates this dynamic beautifully. Abba Lot said to Abba Joseph, "Abba, as far as I can I say my little office, I fast a little, I pray and meditate, I live in peace and as far as I can, I purify my thoughts. What else can I do?"

In answer to Lot's question, Joseph "stood up and stretched his hands towards heaven." As he did so, "his fingers became like ten lamps of fire," and he said to Lot, *"If you will, you can become all flame."*[10]

"All flame." Christianity insists that the destination of the human life is glory. God's glory. Surrendering to the work of the Holy Spirit, we can become aflame with the love and goodness of God. We can be holy as he is holy.

I've seen it with my own eyes. I'm sure you have too. One of the great joys of growing up in the church is that, for all the ugliness I've seen, I've also been witness to the lives of people who were marked by undeniable goodness, beauty, and others-preferring, ego-abandoning, utterly humble and hopeful holiness. People who made knowing God their highest aim in life and became radiant as a result. People whose wisdom and virtue and compassion and joy routinely left me inspired and provoked—that my own life would similarly reflect God's glory.

In the church of my childhood we often said that "God is no respecter of persons." I still believe that. I do not think that this is the special call of a select few. Or that God makes it easier on some than others. I think this is on the table for all of us. I believe that in my bones. We—all of us—can know God. We can, like Jacob, see him in the stuff and substance of our lives. In all the struggle of being human, we can recognize that at the depth of it all, what—no—*whom* we are really "struggling" with is God. And we can be changed by it all, to look more like the God in whose image we are made, who calls us into glory.

THE SHAPE OF THIS BOOK

I want to take you on a journey through what I think are the core movements of the spiritual life. From our first awakenings to God—Father, Son, and Holy Spirit—through inevitable times of spiritual desolation, confusion, and agony, and out into what the psalmist called the "spacious place"[11] of his love and goodness.

Because God, in the Christian imagination, is *triune*—that is, when we say "God," we mean the ongoing, eternally happy relationship that is Father, Son, and Holy Spirit, a relationship that God in his goodness opens up to us, so that we might become sharers of the divine life—I believe that the structure of our spiritual experience is also "triune" in its shape. Which means that the *structure of this book* will also be triune.

In part 1 I want to talk about what it looks like to *come awake* to God the Father, God the Son, and God the Spirit, and to have our lives shaped by that threefold divine reality.

In part 2 I want to give you language for recognizing that same triune presence in the hard places of our lives—where we feel desolate, lost, and agonized. Places where most people abandon the quest. Where the face of the Father is hard to see, where following the Son takes us to places we didn't expect, where the Spirit's presence *burns* and *unmakes* as much as it *quenches* and *soothes*. The make-or-break places.

And in part 3 I want to give you a sense of where, ultimately, God wants to take us—*who* he wants to make us—in and through it all by providing character sketches of three figures from the last one hundred years of church history who lived the journey well, leaving examples for us to follow.

A quick note: Sometimes books on spiritual formation make it seem as though the life of faith is essentially linear. That is, with God's grace and a little of our effort, we can move cleanly from "stage 1" to "stage 2" to "stage 3" and beyond. The whole thing can start to feel a little artificial, and perhaps too *easy*, like making a balsa-wood airplane (does anyone do that anymore?) or building an IKEA chair. *Just do this, then this, then this, and voilà!*

I'm suspicious of books like that. You should be too. The life of faith does not work that way. Like any relationship or organic process, it is a little herky-jerky, even at its beautiful best. So, I am not suggesting that we *first* come awake and *then* "graduate" so as to pass through fire and *then finally* arrive at the state Paul describes in Romans 8. Rather, I am suggesting that in the unpredictability, the *surprise*, of the life of faith, we will often experience all three, together at once, each movement intersecting and coinhering with the others. You might think of it as a spiral. We move around the same axis point (the triune God) but never return to the same place twice, wheeling ever upward and outward toward glory. That, I submit, is what we're signing up for.

I think it's going to be fun. Let's get started.

For each chapter, I'll provide some questions for reflection and a prayer to pray as you digest what you've just read. You'll also find questions for discussion at the end of the book, to aid in processing what you're reading in community.

FOR REFLECTION

What resonates with you about the picture of the spiritual life presented here in the introduction?

PRAYER

Almighty God: Father, Son, and Holy Spirit,
I enter this journey with anticipation.
You see my hope and fear alike.
Take me by my hand.
Lead me into your glory.
Help me trust you through it all.
Amen.

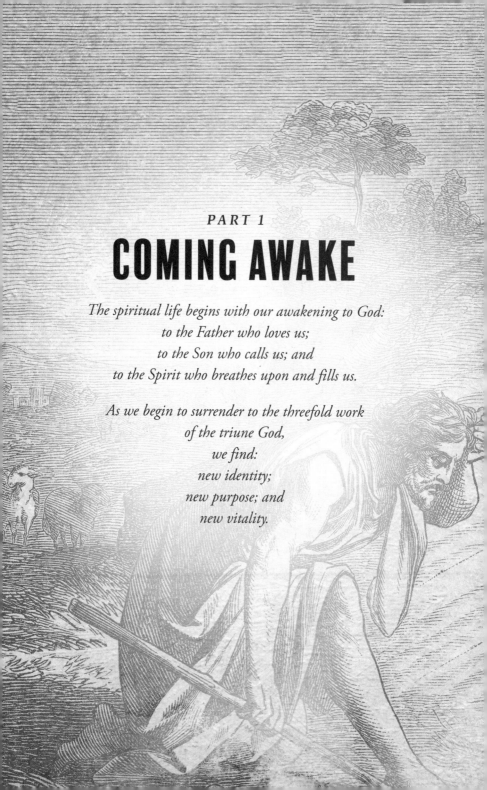

PART 1

COMING AWAKE

The spiritual life begins with our awakening to God:
to the Father who loves us;
to the Son who calls us; and
to the Spirit who breathes upon and fills us.

As we begin to surrender to the threefold work
of the triune God,
we find:
new identity;
new purpose; and
new vitality.

AWAKENING TO THE FATHER

*See what great love the Father has lavished on us, that we should
be called children of God! And that is what we are!*

1 JOHN 3:1

*Jesus has made it clear to me that . . . just as he
has his home with the Father, so do I.*

HENRI NOUWEN, *The Return of the Prodigal Son*

Let's start with the most basic idea of all: To know God at all is
to know him as *Father*. One of the church's oldest confessions
of faith, the Apostles' Creed, says, "I believe in God, *the Father*
Almighty, Creator of heaven and earth."[1] It is, to put it one way,
the church's first term describing God. Who is God? According
to the creed, he is "the *Father* Almighty."

Likewise, to know him as *Father* is to know ourselves as his
children. When God starts making a home in us, forming us
into the persons he desires us to be, one of the first things he
does is this: He plants the dynamic of the Father-child relationship in our hearts. He gives us a name and a place with him and
secures us in his love, answering our primal need to *belong*, to
know that we are not alone.

When I say that the need for this kind of relationship is

"primal," I am saying that it is hardwired into the human frame. If you look around, you'll see it everywhere. There's a reason that videos of military fathers reuniting with their kids get millions of views on Facebook and YouTube. There's a reason people smile when they see toddlers hoisted up on their dads' shoulders, dad and toddler alike grinning ear to ear. There's a reason folks choke up when adult sons and daughters honor their deceased fathers in well-written eulogies. Of course there are equally compelling stories on either side of the relationships between children and mothers, and of course for every such demonstration of father-love there are equally compelling stories of fathering failures. I'd like to suggest that both the resonance and righteous anger we feel at scenes of good and bad fathering are signals of something deeper, something basic to who we are.

A WINDOW INTO DEEP REALITY

"One day," the Gospel of Luke tells us, "Jesus was praying in a certain place. When he finished, one of his disciples said to him, 'Lord, teach us to pray, just as John taught his disciples.'"[2]

Luke's commentary gives us an insight into the disciples' fascination with Jesus. By this time, they had logged enough miles with him to have closely observed at least two things. First, they'd seen the peculiar power and authority with which he conducted his ministry. Teachings and healings and miracles and the marginalized and outcast drawn near and blessed and given a place among the new community forming around him . . . it's no wonder that multitudes flocked to Jesus wherever he went. And the disciples had a front-row seat to the action.

That front-row seat gave them a window into the second

thing: They'd seen the unusual intimacy with which he carried out his relationship with God. Jesus was not simply a solitary, charismatic, supernaturally gifted wonder-worker—and the disciples knew it. No, Jesus was a man who conducted his ministry out of what one of his friends would later call a "closest relationship" with God.[3] The disciples had repeatedly seen the dynamics of this "closest relationship" in action—a public ministry marked by frequent and regular times of withdrawal from the crowds in order to reestablish his communion with God. This was the pattern of the ministry of Jesus. Unusual power grounded in profoundest intimacy. An identity rooted *somewhere*, in *someone* else. And the disciples witnessed it.

I sometimes think about what that must have been like for them. After a busy day of preaching and teaching and healing and driving out demons . . . to be able to retire *with the rabbi himself to a place of prayer*. The access that Jesus gives them to his prayer life is astounding. Luke tells us, in what has to strike our modern ears as at least *odd*, of a time where "Jesus was praying in private *and his disciples were with him.*"[4]

This seems to have been his habit. We get the sense that whatever was happening in Jesus' prayer life, he wanted his disciples to see it. He wanted them to peer through the window of his relationship with God, and there to gaze on the heart of reality. Which is why he gives them full and unconditioned access; he is trying to whet their spiritual appetites as they smell the complex, exquisite savor of his own communion with God.

And they do. Something about it clearly delighted and attracted them, and so on this particular day, they finally just blurt out, "Lord, teach us to pray."

And, as he does so often in the Gospels, Jesus gladly obliges.

WHEN YOU PRAY, SAY . . .

What fascinates me so about this interaction between Jesus and his disciples is the *way in which* Jesus responds to the request. He doesn't give them a long lecture on the theology of prayer. He doesn't lay out for them helpful advice, "tricks of the trade," or four easy steps to getting their prayers answered. He doesn't take them into deep, metaphysical speculations on the return of the soul to its Source in prayer. None of that. With Jesus there is no flight into abstraction.

What he gives them instead are *words*. Bald, bare, unvarnished *words*. "When you pray," he said to them, "say:"

> Father,
> hallowed be your name,
> your kingdom come.
> Give us each day our daily bread.
> Forgive us our sins,
>   for we also forgive everyone who sins against us.
> And lead us not into temptation.[5]

"Do it like this," Jesus says to them. Like a parent teaching a child to ride a bicycle, or a piano teacher instructing a new student in the rudiments of playing properly, Jesus gives concrete, practical instructions. *If you want to know what I know, if you want to see what I see, if you want to experience God the way I experience God, start here: Say these words.*

And the first word of prayer, according to Jesus, is this: *Father.* Everything else he teaches his disciples to pray flows from it and back to it.

I do not think most of us sufficiently appreciate that Jesus poises *Father* as the first word of prayer. Just recently I was leading a worship service where we recited the familiar words of the Lord's Prayer together.[6]

Our Father, we said, *who art in heaven . . .*

We then proceeded to blaze through the list of requests:

Hallowed be . . .

Thy Kingdom . . .

Thy will . . .

Give us this day . . .

Forgive us our trespasses . . .

Lead us not into temptation . . .

We're a charismatic congregation, so—as you might imagine—you could feel the emotion building as we moved through the prayer. By the time we got to the closing affirmation—*Thine is the Kingdom and the power and the glory. For ever and ever. Amen*—praise erupted. It was soul stirring and beautiful.

Now I get it, not every recitation of the Lord's Prayer is as emotional and climactic as what I've just described. (I am also aware that in English, the Lord's Prayer doesn't start with the word *Father* but with *Our;* in Greek, it begins with *Father.*) My point is that it is all too easy to miss the significance of what Jesus is doing in ordering the prayer as he has. We need to learn to stop in order to relish the wonder and gift of the name that Jesus gives us to call the God he knows so well: "Father."

THE GOD JESUS KNEW

It's worth considering that Jesus, being God, could have given his disciples any term of address for God. And surely this is the moment to do it. If you want to help your disciples see God the way you see God, *then every word counts—and the first word most of all.* Don't waste this moment, Jesus. A lot depends on it.

That being the case, he could have told them to call God literally anything. Let's be playful for a minute. If Jesus were a modern spiritual guru, he might have said,

O Great Mystery, who everywhere surrounds us . . .

O Wholly Other, above and beyond us . . .

O Formless Absolute, Ground of Being . . .

O Unknowable One, who is and yet is not . . .

He *could have.* He *didn't.* Instead, he told them to call God "Father."

It turns out that this was one of the things that were new and surprising about Jesus. When you read the Gospels, you cannot escape the conclusion that his *preferred way of talking about God* was "Father."

When exactly he started doing this no one knows, but according to Luke, it began early. In one of the few glimpses of the pre-adult Messiah we have in the Gospels, Luke has a twelve-year-old Jesus sitting in the Temple courts asking the teachers of the Jewish law questions. He and his parents, Luke tells us, had been visiting Jerusalem for the high holy Feast of the Passover, and upon its conclusion, his parents began the journey home to Nazareth, not realizing that the precocious Jesus had stayed behind in Jerusalem.

They traveled, according to Luke, *for an entire day* before realizing their blunder, and then in abject panic hightailed it back to the Holy City—another day's journey—to search for their adolescent son. The next day they found him, engaged in lively theological discussion with Jerusalem's brightest and best.

Luke reports that "everyone who heard him was amazed at his understanding and his answers."[7] Even from a young age, his insight into the character and ways of God was profound. "When his parents saw him," Luke tells us, "they were *astonished*."[8] Obviously. Jesus, separated from his parents for three whole days, seems perfectly confident and comfortable in his surroundings. That is telling. Jesus' relationship with God grounded him, existentially securing him in a way that baffled his parents.

Mother Mary wastes no words in admonishing him: "Son, why have you treated us like this? Your father and I have been anxiously searching for you." And Jesus replies in words that will define the rest of his life: "Why were you searching for me? *Didn't you know I had to be in my Father's house?*" Jesus, even from this young age, lives in an experience of God's fatherhood greater than, encompassing and eclipsing of, his human experience of father- (and mother-) hood. As was so often the case with Jesus, his hearers, Mary and Joseph, "did not understand what he was saying to them."[9]

My Father's house . . . Jesus knew God in a way that others did not. Likewise, Jesus was apparently *anchored in that reality* in a way that no one else was—hence his experience of fearlessness when separated from his human parents. "I had to be in *my Father's house*," he says to Mary and Joseph, adding to their astonishment.

We need to feel the impact of this. None of the Jewish people of Jesus' day knew God like Jesus did. The Old Testament, of course, has its moments of using the imagery of "father-hood" to describe God. Moses said that the Lord carried his people through the wilderness "as a father carries his son."[10] The prophet Isaiah said to God, "You, LORD, are our Father."[11] The Lord himself, speaking from the lips of Jeremiah, says, "I am Israel's father, and Ephraim is my firstborn son."[12] But mostly those references take a back seat to terms of address like *Lord, God Almighty, Lord of Hosts, Rock, Shield, Deliverer*, and of course, the utterly sacred name *Yahweh*—a name so definitive as an identity marker that when God gives it to Moses on Mount Horeb, he states matter-of-factly, "This is my name forever, the name you shall call me from generation to generation."[13]

My name forever . . . It's the Old Testament's version of "Do it like this." So sacred was that name that many Jews of the later Old Testament period, out of reverence, refused to utter it at all, preferring the more generic "Adonai" (Lord) or, simply, "The Name." The message could hardly have been clearer: *This is who God is.*

And then Jesus comes along, and he takes a little-used Old Testament image and makes it the central lens by which we are to know the God he came to reveal. Some 150 times in the canonical Gospels, Jesus refers to God as "Father"—far and away, statistically speaking, his favorite term for God. And when we see him *personally addressing God*, he *only* uses the term "Father."[14] The conclusion is inescapable: God, for Jesus, is "Dad."

But it is the *experience* of "God as Dad" for Jesus that is so unusual. The Gospels make it clear that Jesus experienced God as unambiguously delighted in him, and that he likewise experienced himself as God's happy and adoring child. At the beginning of Jesus' ministry—his baptism in the river Jordan—the divine voice of Yahweh thunders from the clouds in public affirmation, "This is my Son, whom I love; with him I am well pleased."[15] The Father is head over heels for his Son. And the Son returns the love and delight in a ceaseless flow of obedient love. As Jesus says in the Gospel of John, "I always do what pleases him."[16]

The Father in heaven and the beloved Son, Jesus: Here is a relationship that is greater and purer than anything we have ever seen. It is marked by total delight; it is completely free of contempt; it is devoid of envy; it is a perfect and unbroken confluence of wills. Which is why in Christianity we often describe the relationship between the Father and the Son as a "communion"—it is a perfect coming together, an adoring rapport, one with the other, in which there is no hidden agenda, no attempt to wrest the self from the other, no shadow of turning.

Try imagining the spirit of the joyful reunion of the military dad with his kids, written across the entirety of each of their lives, totally unbroken, unstained by ego, selfishness, and fear. *That would be a pale reflection of what the Father shares with his Son, Jesus.* The Father and the Son know themselves in each other. The Father is *the Father of the Son*—knowing himself in the face of his Son. And the Son is *the Son of the Father*—knowing himself in the delight of his Father.

And it is all, always, forever joy.

THE HEART OF REALITY

It is good for us to turn our imaginations as often as we can to the dynamic of the relationship between God the Father and his Son, Jesus—because when we do, we are seeing nothing less than the texture and heart of all reality. God, after all, is the one in whom "we live and move and have our being," according to the apostle Paul.[17] Everything that is exists by and through and unto the relationship between God the Father and Jesus, his Son.

One of the great teachers of the ancient church, St. Augustine, had a very helpful way of talking about this. In a massive treatise on the Trinity, he introduced the term *vestigium trinitatis*— "vestiges of the Trinity." Augustine thought that God—being the God he is—left traces, "vestiges" of his nature in the created order. We might think of them as "signatures" of his character and being. Since the nature of God is Father and Son (in the Holy Spirit), one of the central vestiges discernible in creation is the dynamic between the Father and the Son that I just described.[18]

The created order taken as a whole is perhaps the most obvious example of this. The Father begets the Son from all eternity, and the Son yields his life obediently to the Father from all eternity. The life of the Trinity consists of that movement and flow. *In an analogous way*, creation comes into being by an act of the Father's will and is sustained *as long as he wills it* and *as long as it remains in proper relationship to him*. If the relationship is severed, the creation spins, withers, and dies.

On the *human level*, the stakes are much higher. We also bear the "trace" of the relationship between the Father and the Son, *but so much more than the creation does*—for we have a *choice*. Will we yield our lives to the Father as the Son does? The Scripture teaches us that our first parents, Adam and Eve, did not. And neither do we, their children. The result of this is that we are alienated from the Father and are desperately homesick—though we may not recognize it as such.

HEALING FATHERHOOD

On the human level, the most tragic part of this is the way this sense of alienation touches our relationships with one another. As I drew attention to earlier, many fathers are simply awful to their children—which means that Jesus' words about God's "fatherhood" (or *any* invocation of "parenthood" applied to God) are not easy pills to swallow. Maybe that's you. Maybe your parents were abusive, or distant, or aloof, and your relationship, if you have one at all, is unhealthy, conflicted, or worse—severed completely. Maybe there's a part of you that recoils from the idea of relating to God as "father" because the parent figures in your life were such a disaster.

I cannot tell you how many times as a pastor I have sat with men and women of all ages who chart the beginning of their lives' issues with "Well, my dad . . ." or "Well, my mom . . ." The relationship, for better or for worse, *is* a *vestigium trinitatis*. There's no getting around it. When it breaks down, we spin.

And yet, for as many of those stories as I've heard, for as much anger and bitterness as I've seen, I've also observed that the deepest parts of us ache for the blessing of father and mother. Maybe that's you, too. When you gaze into the relationship between Jesus and his Father, there is a powerful and ineffaceable part of you that longs to find your place in that perfection. You are desperate to know what Jesus knows.

Now—full disclosure here—let me just say that I've been blessed in my own life to come from a long line of great dads.

On the Arndt side of the family, I am the fifth in an unbroken series of firstborn sons. My own oldest son, Ethan, is the sixth. Herman Arndt, Martin Arndt, James Arndt, William Arndt, Andrew Arndt, and Ethan Arndt. A great deal of my own sense of identity comes from the fact that I have a place in that line of those good, decent, godly men. In fact, on my desk I have a picture of myself with my grandpa Jim—me a toothy, beaming six-year-old, leaning back against his chest, with his massive arm around me. It reminds me that I come from somewhere, that I have a name, a place, an identity. I am an *Arndt*.

But here's the thing—being an Arndt who comes from this line of good men is not enough. I'm not saying that *theoretically*, either. I'm saying it *experientially*. Part of the process of spiritual maturity is coming to grips with all of the places in which our family heritage is not and could never be enough. It is learning to recognize where character flaws have been passed on from generation to generation, where sin-stained perceptions of the world have been encoded in our understanding of reality, where things we took for granted as "normal" are—on further review—out of sync with the Kingdom of God. As it turns out, we cannot live by *vestiges* alone.

AWAKENING TO THE FATHER

This is an enormous part of what Christianity means when it talks about "original sin." It is a way of saying that, in my case, none of those Arndt men I've told you about, none of their wives, none of their children, and none of the myriad relationships in the Arndt family stand outside of the need for grace, for redemption. All of those dads—as good as they were—wronged their kids. And so did the moms. And all of the kids in various ways dishonored their dads. And their moms. We are all, the Scriptures teach us, born in sin. Which means that *at our best* we are partial and incomplete in our goodness. *At our worst* we are fatally flawed, even deliberately wicked. Tragically, sin is embedded in our relationships with each other, throwing them off-kilter. The legacy of brokenness given to us by our first parents, Adam and Eve, is passed down from generation to generation. Every human family is sin sick.

One of the beautiful things, therefore, about coming to know *God* as Father is the way in which the experience of *God's* fatherhood gently overwhelms and begins to heal the broken experiences of human family that have marred each and every one of us.

I said earlier that the human father-child relationship is a picture of what the Gospel writers wanted us to see when we think of the inner life of God—the Father and the Son, in the power of the Holy Spirit. But we can't stop there. If we do, we'll wind up with a wrong picture of who God is. The Gospel writers wanted us to see that *the divine life—the Father in the Son and the Son in the Father—is so much better than any human parent-child relationship could ever be.* At one point, Jesus described the relationship between dads and their kids and then concluded his teaching by saying, "If you, then, though you are evil" behave in a kind and gracious way toward your kids, "how much more will your Father in heaven."[19]

The "how much more" is what sets the fatherhood of God on an entirely different level from anything we have seen or experienced in our relationships with one another. Jesus is saying that the human father-child relationship is *at best* a pale reflection of that everlasting union of delight that is the Father and the Son. Which is why right next to the picture on my desk of little Andrew and Grandpa Jim, I have another picture leaning in front of a small wooden cross—the Dutch painter Rembrandt's *The Return of the Prodigal Son*. In it, the bedraggled prodigal—head shaved and draped in threadbare clothing like a slave—buries his head in his elderly father's chest, embraced by the one whose love he had once scorned.

It is a picture not just of *grace* but of a very specific *kind* of grace—the grace of coming home to the Father's house, returning once again to name and place and identity. Henri Nouwen remarks that while the Prodigal Son was in the far country, he "hit the bedrock of his sonship." He notes,

> When he found himself desiring to be treated as one of the pigs, he realized that he was not a pig but a human being, a son of his father. . . . Once he had come again in touch with the truth of his sonship, he could hear—although faintly—the voice calling him the Beloved and feel—although distantly—the touch of blessing.[20]

One of the most profound awakenings I've ever had to the love of the Father came when I was sixteen or so. It was the kind of singular experience of God that leaves a permanent mark on you, changing your whole life. To me, though I'd never really wandered, it felt like a homecoming—like *Knowing you this way, God, is what I was made for*. I have Rembrandt's picture on my desk to remind me that whatever else I learn or experience of God, *I will never graduate beyond the need to "come home" to the Father's love*. It is the original experience of faith—learning to call God "Dad"—and I need to return to it as often as I can. I'll never move beyond it.

And what I find is that when I step into the experience of God's fatherhood, it overwhelms and heals all the places in which being an Arndt was never and could never be enough. I am a better son to my dad, William, and my mom, Nancy, because of my growing experience of God's fathering love. Likewise, I am a better husband to my wife, Mandi, and a better dad to my kids, Ethan, Gabe, Bella, and Liam, because of my growing experience of God's fathering love.

GOD RETURNING US TO GOD

It can do this for you, too. I can't tell you how many times I've seen it. I said earlier that as a pastor, every week I talk to men and women who did not just walk through *deficient* or *defective* experiences with their own fathers (or mothers) but *who suffered in unimaginable ways* at the hands of their human parents. As often as not, the hurt and pain inflicted on these precious people caused their lives to spin wildly out of control as they wandered into the "far country" in search of anything to soothe the pain. *And then*, as the story so often goes, *the fathering love of God found them*, awakened in them a sense of dignity, place, and belonging, led them home, and began to make right all that their biological fathers and mothers had made wrong.

That is what the fathering love of God does to us. It does in us what we cannot do for ourselves—healing and elevating our relationships with one another to the level of his love. It takes the *vestiges* and reconstitutes them inside the reality. As Paul writes in Colossians,

So spacious is he, so expansive, that everything of God finds its proper place in him without crowding. Not only that, but all the broken and dislocated pieces of the universe—people and things, animals and atoms—get properly fixed and fit together in vibrant harmonies, all because of his death, his blood that poured down from the cross.[21]

And that is the *other* reason I have the Rembrandt picture on my desk. I told you that the picture is positioned in front of a small wooden cross. The symbolism is deliberate. When I look at the picture of the prodigal and his father, I know that I am not just seeing *myself* returning home of my own volition. By myself, I can't return home. Neither can you. Only God can do that for us. Only God can return us to God.

The twentieth-century theologian Karl Barth grasped this with astounding clarity. In his discussion of the doctrine of reconciliation, Barth took the parable of the Prodigal Son and gave it a depth of meaning that most of us don't see. For Barth, the entry of Christ Jesus into the world was nothing less than "the way of the Son of God into the far country."[22] Jesus, the eternally obedient Son of the Father, emptied himself of his majesty, taking, as Paul said so beautifully, the form of a servant[23] in order to go into the far country, to find us in our fearful, bedraggled, confused prodigality, and to bring us home to the God he knows, to his Father's house. Barth writes,

> In being gracious to man in Jesus Christ, He [God] also goes into the far country, into the evil society of this being which is not God and against God. He does

not shrink from him. He does not pass him by. . . .
He does not leave him to his own devices. He makes
his situation His own. . . . God is not proud. In His
high majesty He is humble. It is in this high humility
that He speaks and acts as the God who reconciles the
world to Himself.[24]

The journey of Jesus the Son to the Cross, for Barth, was
God's lowering himself to the extreme limits of where our rebel-
lion takes us in order to return us to God. *God brings us home to
God.* And so, when I look at Rembrandt's picture on my desk,
leaning against the cross, I am seeing *at one and the same time*
my own sonship restored *and the Son who has restored it*—and
continues to restore it, with consequences that ramify not only
into my own biological family, but out into the world as well.

That, friend, is a central part of the mystery of "Christ in
us"—which the New Testament talks so often about. Jesus does
not just *show* us the God he knows as "Father." He invites us *to
participate in* the relationship that he has with his Father, and
in so doing, he heals us.

Listen to how Jesus himself put it in his final prayer for his
disciples in John 17:

Righteous Father, though the world does not know
you, I know you, and they know that you have sent me.
I have made you known to them, and will continue to
make you known in order that the love you have for me
may be in them and that I myself may be in them.[25]

It turns out that in making the Father known to us, the love that the Father has for the Son himself is implanted (in ever-increasing measure) in us, *which, for Jesus, seems to be a way of saying that he himself is implanted in us.* We are, beyond all comprehension, *included in that perfect union of love, delight, and harmony that is the relationship between the Father and the Son.*

This is what it means to come awake to God the Father.

FOR REFLECTION

Where do you need to experience God's fatherhood more in your daily life?

PRAYER

Almighty God, heavenly Father,
Thank you for how you have revealed yourself in Jesus.
Teach me to know you like he does,
to experience you like he does,
to trust you like he does.
May your Spirit plant the "Abba" cry in me afresh,
and let the experience of that cry heal my life.
Through Christ the Son,
Amen.

FOLLOWING JESUS, THE LORD

God has made this Jesus, whom you crucified,
both Lord and Messiah.

ACTS 2:36

"It's a dangerous business, Frodo, going out of your door. . . .
You step into the Road, and if you don't keep your feet,
there is no knowing where you might be swept off to."

J. R. R. TOLKIEN, The Fellowship of the Ring

In the person of Jesus Christ, God the Father sojourns in the far country to find us and bring us home. As the Spirit grafts us into the life of the Son, Christ's perfect relationship with the Father becomes our own, gently overwhelming our brokenness, reconciling us in our many alienations, and leading us along paths of healing. We become beloved sons and daughters of God in *the* Son, Jesus Christ. To awaken to this is freedom and joy.

But coming to know Jesus is not simply a means to an end. That is to say, God the Father doesn't just *use* it to accomplish something else; namely, making us his sons and daughters. For Jesus of Nazareth—let us never forget—is *God*. That means that the encounter with him, the person he was and is and ever shall be, adds its own unique dimension to the experience of faith.

But just what is that? What does it mean to encounter Jesus? What is it like to come to know Jesus, really and personally?

THE RADIANT PERSONALITY

I can tell you this for sure—it is bigger than most people realize.

In the middle part of the nineteenth century, a young atheist was serving time in a Siberian prison for his political involvements. Disillusioned, scared, searching, and confined to a cell, the young man read regularly from a copy of the Gospels given to him by the wife of one of his colleagues. Daily he pored over the stories and sayings of Jesus recorded by the Evangelists, Matthew, Mark, Luke, and John. Over time, his atheism was swallowed up by what he described as the "radiant personality of Christ."[1] The glory consumed his unbelief. So compelling was the figure presented to him in the Gospels that he later wrote, "If someone were to prove to me that Christ is outside the truth, then I would prefer to remain with Christ than with the truth."[2]

That young man was the Russian novelist Fyodor Dostoevsky, and for the rest of his life, the radiant personality of Jesus of Nazareth would provide the energy for his writing, lighting the path of his struggle to understand the human condition in famous works such as *Crime and Punishment*, *The Idiot*, and *The Brothers Karamazov*. At the heart of his struggle was the living Christ he encountered in a Siberian prison so many years earlier through his reading of the Gospels. Jesus was his constant and all-encompassing preoccupation.

But just what is it about Jesus that makes him so compelling, so radiant? Why does he still command our attention?

The Catholic writer Flannery O'Connor once described the South, where she grew up, as "Christ-haunted."[3] I love that phrase. *A sense of Jesus hangs in the air. . . .*

Having grown up in the North and now living out in the western United States, I think it is fair to say that in fact *most* of our society is Christ-haunted. What I mean is that while some dismiss Jesus as a fraud or an invention of the church, and while others use his name as a slur, many continue to invoke his name and memory positively. Despite the growing secularization of our culture, it is still not uncommon to hear professional athletes, musicians, actors, or politicians give credit to Jesus for their accomplishments or appeal to the legacy of Jesus as they garner support for their platforms or causes. That *works*, of course, because the name of Jesus still has some measure of "purchase power" in our culture. Truth be told, even our scorn is a measure of how Christ-haunted we are. It is almost as though we are trying to exorcise him from our collective imagination—that luminous and, for many, infuriating figure.

But is this ubiquitous Christ-hauntedness an indication that we really *know* Jesus? I don't think so. I think that as often as not, our culture's familiarity with Jesus is detrimental to hearing and seeing him the way that Dostoevsky, O'Connor, and many others have. Dallas Willard wrote that "familiarity breeds unfamiliarity—unsuspected unfamiliarity," which then, he said, leads to "contempt." He went on to say that "people *think* they have heard the invitation [of Jesus]. They *think* they have accepted it—or rejected it. But they have not. The difficulty today is to hear it at all."[4]

"FOLLOW ME"

For many, the idea that Jesus comes with a call, an invitation, is itself surprising. *I thought Jesus was a figure merely to learn from, or to believe in*, some will say. To be sure, he is those things. But there is more. Jesus is the one who comes to humanity with the urgent call "Follow me."

The call is, quite frankly, startling, disruptive, even demanding. It leaves no room for negotiation or compromise. It carries an undeniable authority. When it penetrates human ears and sinks into human hearts, it does so as a nearly irresistible summons. One of my favorite scenes from the Gospels comes early on and catches the spirit of the call, and its impact, so well:

> As Jesus was walking beside the Sea of Galilee, he saw two brothers, Simon called Peter and his brother Andrew. They were casting a net into the lake, for they were fishermen. "Come, follow me," Jesus said, "and I will send you out to fish for people." At once they left their nets and followed him.
>
> Going on from there, he saw two other brothers, James son of Zebedee and his brother John. They were in a boat with their father Zebedee, preparing their nets. Jesus called them, and immediately they left the boat and their father and followed him.[5]

The manner in which Matthew tells the story is intended to convey the authority and urgency of the call "Follow me." Simon Peter and Andrew leave their nets "at once" to follow him. James and John, the sons of Zebedee, leave the boat and their father "immediately" in response to the call.

What exactly were they signing up for? How long would it last? Would they be able to return to their families and nets? Did they know? Did it occur to them even to ask? Would the mission be dangerous? Does "Follow me" come with health insurance and a 401(k)? Apparently they had no clue. They just responded.

Over and over again in the Gospels, this happens. Jesus comes and summons people, and before they even know exactly what they are being summoned *to*, they respond. Embedded in the call is an authority that makes the heart burn and sets the feet moving before the intellect truly grasps what is happening. Matthew himself was an object of the call: "As Jesus went on from there, he saw a man named Matthew sitting at the tax collector's booth. 'Follow me,' he told him, and Matthew got up and followed him."[6] Just like that.

The late sixteenth- and early seventeenth-century painter Caravaggio captured this scene imaginatively and beautifully in his painting *The Calling of St. Matthew*. Cloaked in the semidarkness and privacy of his little hovel, Matthew's countenance is fixed on a handful of coins on the table in front of him. His life's obsession is the things of this world, which the coins represent. Suddenly Christ appears in the room, lighting it with his presence and pointing a long, demanding finger in Matthew's direction. While Matthew does not immediately look up, his companions do. They know who has appeared and that Matthew's life as he knows it is about to be upended by the call "Follow me."

So it is with Jesus. To encounter him is to be exposed to the all-encompassing voice of the Lord. In Jesus, God calls to us.

The call carries with it little in the way of promises about how things will unfold and where they will finally land. It assures us of little—except that Jesus is with us and that he knows what he is doing. We sense that he is trustworthy, so we take him at his word. Leaving our nets and our boats and our booths, we follow him. And right then and there, the adventure begins.

WHEREVER, WHATEVER

When I first gave my life to Jesus, I remember saying to him, "Wherever you want me, whatever you want, however and whenever you want it—I am all yours." Honestly, I think that kind of response is just what love, in fact, does. If you've ever fallen in love, you know what I'm talking about. Love gives itself, and it gives itself completely. That's what marriage is: *I am yours, and you are mine.* And when the love of Jesus touches us, when his call comes to us, it awakens a similar response—*I am all yours!*

I've spent my life in the church and have had countless conversations with followers of Christ who have heard the call and given themselves to him in exactly this way. They've left (and keep on leaving) safety and security behind because Jesus is calling them to follow, and the level of their obedience routinely staggers me.

Years ago, Mandi and I scheduled a dinner with some folks in a congregation we pastored. Through the grapevine we had heard that they were taking steps toward adoption. With two biological children already, an adoption would be a massive undertaking. We were eager not only to hear the story behind the adoption but to learn how we could help.

"So, has adoption been on your heart for most of your lives?" we asked over dinner.

"Oh yes," the husband replied, "for, like, *weeks*."

He had a good sense of humor. We laughed and then pressed further: "What's the story?"

"Well," his wife replied, "I was in prayer one morning a few weeks ago and was just overcome with the thought that there were kids around the world who had no family to look after them. On my heart especially that morning were children with special needs. I was pleading with Jesus to do something about it when I sensed him saying, 'Okay. Why don't you adopt one?' We talked it over and both felt that the word was genuinely from the Lord, so we decided to take steps to adopt a special-needs child from Africa."

Mandi and I were astonished. Two years later, this couple had adopted not one but two kids from Africa. Both arrived with massive medical needs. Both were and are flourishing because of this couple's obedience. The call came. They responded.

The encounter with Christ the Lord is like that. We say to him, "I am all yours," and what we discover is that he takes those words with uncompromising seriousness. When I said to the Lord all those years ago, "Wherever, whatever, however, and whenever," like most of us, I meant it. I really did. But what I have been surprised at is how often Jesus has come to me, disturbing my safe little world once again with the call "Follow me." It is always startling, like a splash of cold water in the face. I've come to learn that's part of the signature of his call.

Back in 2016, Mandi and I were finishing up our seventh year of ministry at a church in Denver we had helped plant with our friends when we began to feel a bit of disturbance in our hearts. After seven years, the church had really rounded into shape. We were several hundred people strong, with a good leadership team and staff, and money in the bank. Even more than that, we had an identity and reputation and were starting to coach churches and pastors around the country in many of the lessons the Lord had taught us along the way. I loved our work. I loved that church. And I wanted to die there. I could think of nothing better.

And then it happened. Early one morning, I was in prayer and I sensed the Lord say, "Go ahead. Put it on the table."

"Put *what* on the table?" I immediately replied.

"You know what."

"No, I don't," I retorted.

"Yes, you do. Put it on the table."

After a bit of a tussle, I finally blurted out, "My pastorate here, Lord? Would you like to talk with me about that?" Instantly I sensed his smile, which seemed, frankly, crazy to me. After all, getting the church to a place of stability, where it can become a strength and resource to others . . . this is what you work for! This is the destination! The "playbook" says I stay! Plus, Lord, we've already taken the "big risk" in moving here. Haven't we proved that we're obedient? Haven't we graduated? Can we just stop with all the risk and uncertainty now?

Apparently, we hadn't graduated. In fact, I've learned that with Jesus, you never do. You never graduate from the risky and uncertain call "Follow me." Crashing against the shores of our all-too-predictable lives, the call keeps coming, upending everything, making things new.

Within six months, we had resigned and moved on to our next assignment. The adventure continues.

THE LORD JESUS CHRIST

But the question remains: Where does this authority come from? Why is it that when the call of Jesus Christ comes to us, it comes with such urgency? How is it that he can mess up our lives so profoundly?

When Jesus of Nazareth first appeared publicly in ancient Palestine, this was his message: *Repent, for the kingdom of heaven has come near.*[7]

"The kingdom of heaven has come near" was Jesus' shorthand way of talking about how Israel's God, whom he called Father, was on the move in a fresh way, righting wrongs and restoring what had been broken by sin. The ancient promises were coming to fruition, the dreams of Israel's prophets were being realized, the time of fulfillment was at hand.

There were others, of course—most notably Jesus' cousin John the Baptist—who preached this message.[8] In truth, the message itself—in terms of content—was simply a summary of all that the prophets of Israel had prophesied. There was nothing novel in it. What was it, then, that marked Jesus as different? What was it that made him so compelling to so many, so quickly?

Theologian Wolfhart Pannenberg hits the nail on the head here. He says that Jesus' Kingdom preaching—though similar in content to the preaching of others—was distinguished by at least three things:

First, he says, Jesus did not describe a *path* to the future but brought the future's urgency to bear on the people by issuing a call: Repent. The call to repent is an invitation to change your thinking—and your whole life as a result. In other words, whereas Old Testament figures like Isaiah, Jeremiah, Ezekiel, and Daniel painted pictures of God's intended future in elaborate detail and sought, as they were led by the Spirit, to describe how and in what way their hearers could begin to move toward it, Jesus declared that the future was *now*, and that it was time to do something about it: repent.

But second—and here is what really marked Jesus as different—Pannenberg says that Jesus made *himself* the focal point of his Kingdom preaching. "For this reason," he writes, "the future participation in salvation was decided by the attitude taken toward his person."[9]

This is crucial. The Gospel records are clear that though John the Baptist preached the same message as Jesus, John ultimately pointed people *away* from himself.

> Finally they said, "Who are you? Give us an answer to take back to those who sent us. What do you say about yourself?"
>
> John replied in the words of Isaiah the prophet,
> "I am the voice of one calling in the wilderness,
> 'Make straight the way for the Lord.'"[10]

John called people to ready themselves for Jesus; Jesus, on the other hand, called people to follow him. The implication could hardly have been clearer: *The future is now; follow me, and you will step right into it. Refuse me, and you will miss it entirely.*

And that leads to the third thing Pannenberg says distinguished Jesus: namely, that he did not *disclose* the end of history but rather *presented the end in his own person.*[11]

Jesus is King and Kingdom all wrapped up into one. This is the reason why his message and preaching came and still come with such compelling urgency and authority. In him we are meeting both incarnate God and the Future-in-Person of the Father's intention for every human being; indeed, for the entirety of his beloved world. He is True God and True Man, both at once and entirely—one and the same Jesus Christ our Lord. This is what made and still makes Jesus so compelling.

HE MUST BE MORE

While in seminary in the Chicagoland area, I worked as a host at a restaurant. One of my coworkers was a young woman who had been born and raised in a secular home. At the time, she was a sophomore in college, attending a local Catholic university. She knew I was a seminary student, and so one day she asked me a question:

"Hey, so you're pretty familiar with the Bible, right?"

"Yes," I replied. I already liked where this conversation was headed.

"Well, I'm taking this class on the Gospels, and we're reading that big block of Jesus' teaching in Matthew . . ."

"The Sermon on the Mount?" I asked.

"Yeah, that's it," she said. "Well, you know that part where Jesus says if you don't *actually* commit adultery but do it in your heart, it's basically the same as actually committing it? Well, I've *always* believed that! It's crazy to see him teach it!" At this point, she was gushing.

"That's really cool," I said. "Sounds like this class has been a good experience for you."

"Oh yeah," she said. "Amazing. I keep having moments just like that one, where I read the Gospels and think, *How can he be so* right?"

I loved every second of what was happening but didn't want to spook her by seeming overanxious. So I tried to play it cool.

"You know," I said, "I've been reading the Gospels and following Jesus my whole life, and I still have regular moments like that. What is more, I'm guessing that at some point soon you're going to be reading the Gospels and you're going to find yourself thinking, *He must be more than a man.*"

Her eyes widened. "I think that's already starting to happen," she said.

"More than a man." That's the New Testament's claim about Jesus. That he is God-in-Flesh, walking among us, teaching us, calling us to surrender our lives to him.

The early followers of Jesus captured his divine-human identity succinctly and powerfully by calling him "Lord Jesus Christ." In so doing, they were making three crucial identifications:

First, to call him "Lord" was to identify him with Yahweh of the Old Testament, who was sovereign over heaven and earth. "The earth is the LORD's," the psalmist said, "and everything in it, the world, and all who live in it."[12] Giving expression to a fundamental Old Testament belief, the psalmist claimed that everything that was and is and ever shall be belongs to Yahweh. And though Yahweh's universal sovereignty was largely unrecognized, the prophet Zechariah spoke of a day when "the LORD will be king over the whole earth. On that day there will be one LORD, and his name the only name."[13] And so when the early believers called Jesus "Lord," they were saying that what was true of Yahweh was also true of Jesus—namely, that he was sovereign over all and one day would be recognized as such. Astounding.

To call him "Christ," on the other hand, was to identify him as the Messiah of the Jews. When the great Old Testament poets and prophets envisioned the overthrow of evil and the enthronement of Yahweh, they frequently positioned this event as *taking place through a human agent*—an "anointed one" (that is what the Greek *Christos* and the Hebrew *Messiah* both mean) who would usher in the Kingdom of God. Speaking by the Spirit, one of Israel's greatest human leaders, King David himself, peered into the future and beheld someone greater than he who would come to make the enemies of God a footstool for his feet:

The LORD [Yahweh] says to my lord:

"Sit at my right hand
   until I make your enemies
   a footstool for your feet."[14]

This is as good a description of the Messiah as you will find in the Old Testament. And it just so happens to be the single most quoted psalm in the New Testament, for it describes a future human agent to whom the enemies of God would submit. One of Jesus' best friends, Peter, quotes this psalm during the first "Christian" sermon ever preached (Acts 2) and says that the resurrection of Jesus was evidence of Yahweh's approval of this man: "Therefore let all Israel be assured of this," Peter says, "God has made this Jesus, whom you crucified, both Lord and Messiah"[15]—sovereign God and sovereign Man all at once. We begin to see why his call to "follow me" carries such profound weight.

And that brings us to the last identification of this person—that he is Jesus. He was and is and ever shall be the Lord *Jesus* Christ. One of the things that astonishes me about the Gospels is how the writers insist that for all of his divinity, *Jesus is and will forever remain the particular, human person that he is.* The early Christians, in the midst of their ever-growing understanding of the divine identity of the Son of God, never stopped calling him by the name the angel gave his human parents, Mary and Joseph: *Jesus*, the one who would save his people from their sins.[16]

Jesus—born of the virgin
Jesus—raised by Joseph and Mary in Nazareth of Galilee
Jesus—son and brother and friend

Jesus—of the house and line of David
Jesus—baptized by his cousin John in the Jordan River
Jesus—who began his public ministry in the fifteenth year of the Roman ruler Tiberius Caesar

Jesus—who healed the blind and raised the dead
Jesus—who touched lepers and outcasts
Jesus—who knew anger and pain and hunger and suffering

Jesus—who proclaimed the now-and-coming Kingdom of God
Jesus—who recruited men and women into the revolutionary movement of his disciples

Jesus—whose words and actions provoked bloodthirsty anger and hostility

Jesus—who was crucified under Pontius Pilate, died, and was buried; who descended to the dead

Whatever else the early church believed about the Lord Christ, it knew it could never leave behind his peculiar, particular human identity. The one who was *Lord* and *Messiah* never stopped being the human *Jesus* whom they knew and loved during the days of his earthly ministry. The resurrected Christ himself was adamant that they understand this. One of the most fascinating and telling Resurrection scenes in the Gospels occurs in Luke. The disciples are gathered, still trying to puzzle out the events of the previous days:

> While they were still talking about this, Jesus himself
> stood among them and said to them, "Peace be with you."
> They were startled and frightened, thinking they saw
> a ghost. He said to them, "Why are you troubled, and
> why do doubts rise in your minds? Look at my hands
> and my feet. It is I myself! Touch me and see; a ghost
> does not have flesh and bones, as you see I have."
> When he had said this, he showed them his hands
> and feet. And while they still did not believe it because
> of joy and amazement, he asked them, "Do you have
> anything here to eat?" They gave him a piece of broiled
> fish, and he took it and ate it in their presence.[17]

"Thinking they saw a ghost." I love that. They also were "Christ-haunted." The resurrected one reassures them: "It is I myself! Touch me and see!" It is really, truly, always and forever the man Jesus, exalted in his resurrection from the dead. And then, as if the invitation to touch him and see weren't enough, *he asks for a piece of fish and eats it in their presence.* The early Christians did not believe—though some tried to make it so—that his divine, exalted status was something he possessed *in spite of* his particular, human identity, or in a way that overrode his human identity. No, it was "as this man," so they understood, "Jesus is God."[18]

Forever.

INTO HIS STORY

Part of what all of this meant for the early believers was that the *unique manner* in which the now-resurrected and ascended Christ exercised his rule carried the same signature as the manner of that exercise during the days of his earthly ministry. Namely, that *just like he had* at the shore of the Sea of Galilee, *just like he had* on the dusty roads of ancient Palestine, *just as he had* in the Temple courts of Jerusalem, *so he was doing now*—calling men and women to join him in his movement, *which was nothing less than the restoration of all things.* It was the call for men, women, and children everywhere to take their little stories and link them up with the large story that God was telling through him in the world.

This is what I mean when I say that we need to hear the message and invitation of Jesus afresh. For many people in our culture, if the name of Jesus is not dismissed out of hand, treated as the punch line of a joke, or used as profanity, it is typically little more than a yard ornament in a life that is more or less already put together. Jesus is simply part of the furniture; a quaint bit of spiritual decoration for life as we already know it.

But if what we are saying about Jesus here is true, then that is the very last thing he can be. The call of Jesus now is the same as it was two thousand years ago—to leave everything we know behind to join the rollicking company of those who are following Jesus in his liberating, healing, world-transforming ministry. It is still and always the call to "follow me"—a call that demands a reevaluation of our whole lives, which most of us are rather unwilling to do.

I was struck powerfully by this one Easter morning some years ago. Awake and preparing for our church's Easter service, I happened to catch a news clip of a major world leader talking blithely about the beauty of Easter. The leader waxed eloquent on the legacy of Jesus and the importance of learning from his teaching and imitating his example—all good things, mind you. But nowhere to be found was any sense of Easter as an invitation to give our lives to the living Lord Jesus Christ, who personally and powerfully addresses each and every one of us. As I watched this leader, I thought, *Do you actually believe what you're saying? If the message of Easter is true, then there's no way to remain calm, cool, or collected about it. If Jesus is Lord, if his Kingdom will one day overwhelm our little kingdoms, then we'd all better stop talking and start aligning* now!

I am suggesting that we recover an appropriate sense of urgency when it comes to Jesus. Humanity is being summoned by the Lord of heaven and earth, the man Jesus Christ. God is speaking. And we are being called not to align *him* with *our lives* (which is what so many do), but to align *our lives* with *his rule and reign* as the one who is both *Lord* and *Christ*. This will

demand a new valuation of everything that we are and everything that we have. We will, as the disciples did two millennia
ago, have to leave life as we know it behind to follow Jesus . . .
in whatever it is he is doing in the world.

And he is doing much. Just as he was in the first century,
today he is healing blind eyes, welcoming outcasts, breaking
the rod of the oppressor, challenging the rich and powerful,
responding to the needs of the poor and the destitute, and ush-
ering in the Kingdom. When we hear and respond to the call of
Jesus, we become partners with him in this ongoing ministry of
justice, healing, and reconciliation. The voice of the Lord summons us into it, making our lives more than they ever would
have been on their own.

What else explains the boldness of the early apostles or the
courage of the martyrs? What else explains St. Patrick's mission
to evangelize his oppressors or St. Francis of Assisi's appeals
to the powerful in an effort to end the Crusades? What else
explains William Wilberforce's determination to stop the slave
trade or Martin Luther King Jr.'s intrepid preaching in the face
of the Ku Klux Klan? What else explains the behavior of believers who, at great personal risk and cost, have left safety and
comfort behind to reach the unreached, to plant churches and
to found mission organizations, to build hospitals, orphanages,
and halfway houses; who, personal comfort notwithstanding,
have welcomed orphans and foster children and widows into
their homes, looked after the sick, suffering, and dying, turned
the other cheek and gone the extra mile and prayed for those
who despitefully use them?

What explains this gutsy, bizarre, beautiful behavior?

It is, I suggest, the personal call of the Lord Jesus Christ.

"ACCEPTING" JESUS?

I think by now it should be obvious that this is bigger than
simply believing some true things about Jesus. It is even bigger
than "accepting Jesus into your heart." I know that many in the
church today talk that way. This is probably one of the reasons
the world is comfortable treating Jesus like a yard ornament.
We tell people that if they simply believe X, Y, and Z about
Jesus and *receive* or *accept* him into their hearts, then they will
find favor with God, and all will be well in the end. *The problem with that is that it leaves your life as you know it more or less
intact*—and, as we have seen, this is the one thing that the call
of Jesus never does.

Now, is there biblical precedent for this kind of talk?
Absolutely. Here's what the apostle Paul wrote to the believers
living in Rome:

> If you declare with your mouth, "Jesus is Lord," and
> believe in your heart that God raised him from the
> dead, you will be saved. For it is with your heart that
> you believe and are justified, and it is with your mouth
> that you profess your faith and are saved.[19]

But notice: There it is again—*the Lord Jesus!* Paul was not
telling the Roman believers to give easy mental assent to some
"spiritual truths" so that they could find right standing with
God. He was telling them, *If your whole heart is convinced that
the God of Israel really did raise up and exalt Jesus as Lord, and if
you are willing to acknowledge it publicly, accepting his call and*

joining his movement, whatever it costs you—then, friend, you are on the right side of history. You are and will be saved.

And cost it did. Many early followers of Jesus, during the first few centuries of the church, suffered terribly at the hands of family, friends, and local authorities for their allegiance to Jesus. It's worth asking: Why did anyone stay with it?

New Testament scholar Larry Hurtado tackles this exact question in a fabulous little book entitled *Why on Earth Did Anyone Become a Christian in the First Three Centuries?* He asks the question because his work as a historian of the early church revealed to him just how high the cost of becoming a follower of Jesus was. If the benefits of following Jesus didn't outweigh the costs, Hurtado argues, it wouldn't be worth continuing. So what were those benefits? Why on earth would anyone become a Christian? Or *stay* a Christian?

After surveying the relevant source material, he concludes with this (remember, he's writing as a historian trying to deal objectively with the facts):

> It is clear to me that early Christian allegiance was
> not solely acceptance of a set of beliefs intellectually
> considered, *but involved also the affective and inter-*
> *personal impact of those beliefs*. . . . I think that we
> must allow [this] some genuine and significant
> role in accounting for their readiness to take up
> Christian commitment, and for the resolve of those
> who maintained that commitment in the face of
> the difficulties that it entailed.[20]

The "affective and interpersonal" that he describes there is nothing less than the person of Jesus Christ. That is, *the early Christians believed they had really and truly encountered God in Jesus*—the God who loved them, forgave them, and had called them into his purposes. Because they believed that in Jesus *it was God with whom they were dealing*, and that this God loved them and was totally committed to them, they likewise *gave* themselves totally to following him—wherever it took them, whatever it cost them.

For Hurtado, the classic example of this is Paul, whose conversion experience on the Damascus road (detailed in Acts 9) was not a matter of "accepting" Jesus into his heart the way we usually think of it. Rather, it was an encounter with the risen Christ, which threw him to the ground and blinded him temporarily so that he could see the world with healed eyes. Saul (who later became Paul) was literally upended. This experience would shape the rest of his life, leading him to the most radical kinds of obedience and self-giving. Listen to his words in Philippians:

> Whatever were gains to me I now consider loss
> for the sake of Christ. What is more, I consider
> everything a loss because of the surpassing worth
> of knowing Christ Jesus my Lord, for whose sake I
> have lost all things. I consider them garbage, that I
> may gain Christ and be found in him, not having
> a righteousness of my own that comes from the
> law, but that which is through faith in Christ—the
> righteousness that comes from God on the basis of
> faith. I want to know Christ—yes, to know the power

of his resurrection and participation in his sufferings, becoming like him in his death, and so, somehow, attaining to the resurrection from the dead.[21]

Paul, gripped by the beauty and power of the Lord Christ, desires to give his whole life away in the service of seeing the Kingdom come and the will of God done on earth as it is in heaven. As he does, he experiences a power that takes him *way* out beyond his old identity and into new identity, purpose, and meaning. Responding to the call of Jesus places him in the horizon of resurrection—the dawn of God's new world.

"SWEPT OFF" INTO THE KINGDOM

That, friend, is what the encounter with Jesus looks like. It is not simply about believing. It is about *what believing in him for who he is—the world's true Sovereign and Lord—does to us, making us fellow journeyers with him on the rollicking adventure of salvation.* That's what the New Testament means when it talks about the *obedience* of faith.[22]

And this is not for the spiritually "elite" alone. There are no spiritually elite with God. There is only the mass of men and women, sinners each and all, who have and are together responding to the call of Christ, "Follow me," and are willing to go with him wherever he leads.

In this sense, I think, we're a little like J. R. R. Tolkien's hobbits. Frodo, Sam, Merry, and Pippin are called into a quest that will demand their whole lives. It is bigger than any of them. But they have a part to play. Having departed the comfortable confines of Hobbiton, when the hobbits reach the edge of the

Shire, Sam looks out "across lands he had never seen," wrote Tolkien, "to a new horizon." Just then, Frodo begins to recite an old rhyme:

> *The Road goes ever on and on*
> *Down from the door where it began.*
> *Now far ahead the Road has gone,*
> *And I must follow, if I can,*
> *Pursuing it with weary feet,*
> *Until it joins some larger way,*
> *Where many paths and errands meet.*
> *And whither then? I cannot say.*

Pippin remarks, "That sounds like a bit of old Bilbo's rhyming. . . . It does not sound altogether encouraging." Frodo replies, "Certainly it reminds me very much of Bilbo. . . . He used often to say there was only one Road; that it was like a great river: its springs were at every doorstep, and every path was its tributary. 'It's a dangerous business, Frodo, going out of your door,' he used to say. 'You step into the Road, and if you don't keep your feet, there is no knowing where you might be swept off to.'"[23]

Scary and not altogether encouraging indeed. But this will be the adventure that gives their lives meaning and purpose they never would have had on their own.

Just like ours.

FOR REFLECTION

Are there places you sense Jesus calling you to? What are they? What stands between you and following Jesus there?

PRAYER

Lord Jesus Christ, Son of the Father,
Help me recognize:
your now-and-coming lordship,
your all-encompassing claims,
and your personal call to me.
Give me courage:
to answer your call,
to go where you lead,
and to daily allow myself to be swept off my feet by the
*   adventure of following you.*
Amen.

FILLED WITH THE SPIRIT

You will receive the gift of the Holy Spirit.

ACTS 2:38

We believe in the Holy Spirit,
the Lord, the Giver of Life.

THE NICENE CREED

Ready to make the next move? In chapter 1 we talked about the experience of awakening to the Father, letting his love overwhelm and heal our brokenness. In chapter 2 we talked about learning to surrender our whole lives to the Lord Jesus Christ, hearing and obeying his startling call, "Follow me." So far, that's two of the three members of what Christians refer to as "the Trinity." *Father, Son,* and now—Holy Spirit.

What is it like to come to know God the Holy Spirit? What does the Holy Spirit *do*?

Sometimes I think that the Holy Spirit is the most misunderstood and underappreciated member of the Trinity. God the Father seems to be an idea that a lot of people can wrap their minds around, a sort of all-powerful dad-like figure who runs the universe. God the Son would in theory be a bit more challenging ("God has a *kid*?") *except* that in the Gospels, we have the earthly life of Jesus of Nazareth to look at, making the concept more concrete.

And then we come to the *Holy Spirit*. What are we talking about here? A numinous, sacred cloud? A divine mist or a vapor? The language that the older versions of the Bible used for this mysterious third member of the Trinity was "Holy *Ghost*." Even worse. An apparition. Who would want a relationship with *that*?

Complicating matters is the fact that the way some Christians talk makes it seem as if the Holy Spirit is the member of the Trinity responsible only for the most bizarre aspects of the Christian life. I know this—laying all my cards on the table here—because I grew up in a "charismatic" church, meaning that we believed in signs and wonders and miracles and gifts of the Spirit. In my mind, God the Father oversaw the cosmos, God the Son taught us how to live, and died and rose again to give us new life, and God the Holy Spirit did . . . well . . . *everything else*—mostly all the wild and crazy stuff that happened in church. In the triune division of labor, the Spirit was responsible for the fantastical.[1]

Many Christians, it seems to me, whether they are tongue-talking charismatic, anti- or noncharismatic, or somewhere in between, tend to feel that way. I had a friend some years ago who grew up in a Christian household that embraced a studied indifference to all things Spirit-related. She and her husband had just started attending our church and were grateful for the way we talked openly, warmly, and biblically about the Holy Spirit. Over coffee, she related this to me about her upbringing: "For us, the Holy Spirit was like the weird third wheel of the Trinity, or like the strange uncle you run into every so often at family reunions. We just didn't talk about the Spirit at all."

I laughed out loud. But it really is so sad, because the experience of the Holy Spirit, as we will see, is not just beautiful; it is essential to our rising into all God is and has for us.

WHEN GOD BREATHES

The tumultuous events of the weekend had left them completely depleted. The disciples had betrayed and abandoned their friend and leader, Jesus, leaving him defenseless against the bloodlust of the religious leaders and the angry mob. Crucified, dead, and buried, the story of Jesus—and all the hope and promise it entailed—as far as they could see, was over.

Until that morning of the first day of the week. One of their number, Mary Magdalene, had gone to the tomb to anoint Jesus' body with spices. Upon arriving, she noticed that the stone with which the tomb was sealed had been rolled away from the entrance. Looking inside, Mary—to her horror—saw that the body of Jesus had gone missing. To the injury of the Crucifixion now was added the insult of a likely grave robbery.

Afraid, panic-stricken, and aggrieved, Mary ran back to her friends with the news. Two of them came with her to verify her report. Sure enough, the body was indeed missing. They wandered back to where they were staying, bewildered.

Mary, meanwhile, remained behind in the garden by the tomb, weeping. And there, in her grief and alarm, he met her. At first she thought he was the gardener, but as the conversation unfolded, suddenly she recognized him—Jesus, the Lord, her dear friend. "Do not hold on to me," he told her, "for I have not yet ascended to the Father. Go instead to my brothers and tell them, 'I am ascending to my Father and your Father, to my God and your God.'"[2]

Can you imagine the surge of energy Mary must have felt? Doing exactly what Jesus had told her to do, Mary made a beeline back to the disciples with the report "I have seen the Lord!"[3] It had to have been at once invigorating and confusing and terrifying to them. What could any of it mean?

In the midst of their confusion and terror, John reports this:

> On the evening of that first day of the week, when the
> disciples were together, with the doors locked for fear
> of the Jewish leaders, Jesus came and stood among
> them and said, "Peace be with you!" After he said this,
> he showed them his hands and side. The disciples were
> overjoyed when they saw the Lord.
>
> Again Jesus said, "Peace be with you! As the Father
> has sent me, I am sending you." And with that he
> breathed on them and said, "Receive the Holy Spirit." [4]

The risen Christ appears to them, amid their fear and doubt, speaking a word of peace, wrapping them into the mission given to him by his Father. The same one who had called to them along the shores of the Sea of Galilee was calling to them again, here and now, on the far side of death. The mission, so it turned out, would continue.

But note what Jesus does immediately after commissioning them: He *breathes* on them and says, "Receive the Holy Spirit."

The obvious implication seems to be that the disciples cannot do or be any of the things that Jesus intends for them to do or be apart from the experience of the Spirit of God. And this is confirmed by what Jesus says in the book of Acts. Just before his ascension into heaven, Jesus tells his disciples, "Do not leave Jerusalem, but wait for the gift my Father promised, which you have heard me speak about. For John baptized with water, but in a few days you will be baptized with the Holy Spirit."[5]

And indeed, a few days later, that is exactly what happened. The second chapter of Acts tells the story. The disciples, gathered together for prayer, hear a sound like the blowing of a violent wind and see tongues of fire separating and descending on each one of them, filling each of them with the Holy Spirit. This immersive experience of the Third Person of the Trinity spills out into the streets, where Peter begins preaching to a group of astonished onlookers, telling them the good news that the one crucified was now raised to life, offering the gift of the Spirit to all who would receive. Three thousand people were added to their number that day, and the church was born. Of that moment, we are all the beneficiaries.

But note what it was predicated on: the Holy Spirit.

God breathed his Spirit. And the dead came to life.

SPIRIT OF LIFE

I'm a pretty consistent devotional guy. Most mornings consist of a fairly predictable and stable routine: wake up, get the coffee going, brush my teeth, throw on a sweatshirt and a baseball cap, grab my Bible and a cup of the sacred brew, and (when weather permits) head out to the front porch.

I live in Colorado, so perhaps I have a bit of an unfair advantage here, but my goodness, something about starting my day outdoors in God's good creation, pulling deep draughts of the fresh air into my lungs, absorbing the artistic miracle that is the ever-changing color palette of the morning sky . . . it just works wonders for my soul.

I typically take a bit of time just to center myself, sipping a bit of that coffee as I come awake to the rustle of the gentle breeze dancing in the treetops, the soft light coming from the eastern horizon, and the early sounds of morning in the neighborhood.

There, in that place of growing centeredness, I give thanks. For whatever comes to mind: sleep and coffee and sights and sounds and smells and my family and my work and the gift of awareness and the joy of friendship with Jesus. My thoughts start to come into focus, and my heart begins to fill.

I open the Scriptures. Poring over the pages of sacred text, I ask for the light of revelation. That Jesus, the Teacher, would walk alongside me through the countryside of Scripture, show-ing me his name and face everywhere. I also ask for the grace of obedience. That what I'm learning and seeing wouldn't fall by the wayside but would be worked into the stuff and substance of my life. I pray in and through and around it all, trying to bathe my life and the world in which I live in the testimony of Scripture.

Generally, I journal a bit about what I've seen and experi-enced. Sometimes, when it's all a little too large for prose, I write poetry about it, or prayers. I've brushed up against the ineffable God. Somehow, I feel, that experience must be recorded, how-ever feebly I am able to.

There are times when the experience of God in those spaces is powerful and profound. My mind lights with fresh truth, my spirit soars with praise, and tears fall down my face. Other times—much more often, actually—it is all very subtle, like the sound of the breeze in the treetops. If you weren't paying attention, you'd miss it.

Either way, in whatever form it comes, it strengthens and refreshes me. The love of the Father washes into me again. Devotion to Jesus arises again. I know that my life isn't my own. I've been claimed by God and sent into his world with blessing. I am an ambassador of the Kingdom.

I want to suggest that the entire experience I have just described to you is an experience of the Spirit. *Any time* we brush up against the life of God, we are brushing up against none other than God the Holy Spirit.

Listen to how the writer of Genesis opens the drama of Creation:

> In the beginning God created the heavens and the
> earth. Now the earth was formless and empty, darkness
> was over the surface of the deep, and the Spirit of God
> was hovering over the waters.
>
> And God said, "Let there be light," and there was
> light.[6]

The Genesis text gives us—like the flash of a strobe light—a brief and tantalizing glimpse of the Great Protagonist of the Creation epic. With the eyes of faith, Christian preachers, exegetes, and theologians have looked back into the text of Genesis 1:1-3 and seen the three primary divine characters of the biblical story at work. We have:

- **God the Father,** the Almighty, the maker of heaven and earth, of all that is, seen and unseen[7] (*In the beginning God created the heavens and the earth. . . .*);
- **God the Word,** which, as the prophet Isaiah said, does not "return . . . void" but accomplishes all that the Father sends it to accomplish,[8] who would one day be enfleshed in Jesus (*And God said, "Let there be light," and there was light. . . .*); and
- **God the Holy Spirit,** brooding over the terrible, watery darkness (*and the Spirit of God was hovering . . .*).

As we read, we are already on the edges of our seats: *God is about to do something.*

Now the word that the ancient Hebrew writer uses for "Spirit" is *ruach*. (If you want to know how to pronounce *ruach*, just pretend like you're trying to clear something out of the back of your throat when you get to the "*ch*." Good job.) It's important to know that *ruach* in the Old Testament doesn't just mean "spirit" the way that we normally think of it: as something *less than really real*, something *shadowy, vague,* and *opaque.* Accordingly, when people in our day use the word "*spirit*ual," there tends to be an assumption that what we're talking about does not carry that much relevance for "real life."

That, of course, is a modern bias that is totally foreign to the biblical mind. For the Bible writers, *ruach* has *everything* to do with "real life." In fact, *ruach* is what makes "real life" *life at all.* You see, *ruach* carries a range of meaning that includes not just what we might think of as "spirit" but also *breath* (recall the text from John 20) and *wind* (recall the text from Acts 2)—both, in their way, very "lively" things.

So, when we talk about the divine *ruach*, we're not talking about a "less-than-something." We're talking about an invisible but very real and present power that has a dramatic influence on what we normally think of as "real life."

That being the case, I tend to think that the entire range of the meaning of the word *ruach* is present here in this early glimpse into the character and ways of God that we see in Genesis. The writer is giving us a full-bodied sense of what God is up to. The *ruach* of God is:

- the "wind" of God that blows over the waters, stirring them up in a way that sets the stage for God's creative work;
- the "breath" of God exhaled over the waters, beginning to fill the deathly void with life; and
- the "spirit" of God that flutters over the waters, teeming with God's animating power.

Here's what is crucial to see. What binds these three dimensions of meaning together is, quite simply, *life*. God's Spirit is the Spirit of *Life*. Even better, God's Spirit is *God's Life* or, we might say, *God's Vitality*. One of the early church fathers, St. Ambrose, said, "Just as the Word of Life is Life, so the Spirit of life is Life."[9] Another church father, St. Basil the Great, said, "He lives . . . [because] he is the source of life."[10] God's life. He is the Spirit of the Living God, the Life Breath of the Almighty.

Think about it for a moment. On the human level, when our "spirit" departs, what happens? When our "breath" departs, what happens? Our *ruach* within us just *is* our life, in the same way that God's *ruach* within God is God's own Life.

Even more, as the writer of Genesis tells us, in the creative action of God, the *ruach* does not just stay within Godself. If we'll pay attention to the movements of Genesis, we will notice that the *ruach* flows out *beyond* Godself into the created order. Listen to how theologian Robert Jenson puts it:

> The "*ruach* of the Lord" is the Lord's *breath*, the
> whirlwind of his *liveliness* that agitates whatever he turns
> toward. . . . The Lord's Spirit is his life as he transcends
> himself to enliven other reality than himself.[11]

This is *precisely* what we see happening in Genesis. The earth was "formless and empty" with a deep, penetrating, palpable darkness over the face of the watery depths—and even there, exactly there, the *ruach* of God was present. The Life of God was about to break forth—God, as Jenson puts it, "transcend[ing] himself to enliven other reality than himself." The almighty God uttered his creative Word in and through his Breath,[12] and the creation began to take shape. Light and life broke into darkness and death.

Like it did to the disciples gathered in fear.

Like it did at Pentecost.

Like it always does when God breathes.

COME, HOLY SPIRIT

This is the reason that one of the oldest prayers of the church is the simple prayer "Come, Holy Spirit." It is a prayer that anyone can pray, anywhere. When we pray it, we are inviting the life-giving *ruach* to come and do what only the *ruach* can—to descend on us as the whirlwind of God's liveliness, to awaken us to the reality of God, even to agitate us in the effort to drive death out of our lives. When the Spirit is breathed on us, we live.

A man began attending our church some years ago. He was not a believer, though he was open to God. Up to that point, his life had been inexpressibly difficult. A tumultuous childhood, confusing teenage years, the meteoric rise and fall of a business he had started as a young man, and a cancer diagnosis for his wife, to which—after a long and grueling battle that coincided with the demise of the business—she eventually succumbed.

When he wandered into our church, by his own admission, he was numb. Dead inside. His circumstances had left him gutted. And yet, he came. Week after week he sat in our gatherings, singing with us, listening to stories of Jesus, coming to the table of the Lord. Over time, something began to crack.

We sat together one day as he related to me, "I'm not sure what's happening to me. But I'm coming to your church, and I'm feeling things I've never felt before. I cry through most of the services. I feel the love and the welcome of these people, and it just overwhelms me. The stories of Jesus just move me so. I feel drawn in. And I also feel like something is being drawn *out*. It's like all the pain and hurt and confusion of my past is being brought out into the light. It hurts like crazy, but I think it's good. *What's happening to me?*"

"I'll tell you what's happening," I said. "You're experiencing the Holy Spirit. This is what the Spirit does. Keep running with it."

God, by his Spirit, was bringing life to this man's desolation, as only God by his Spirit can. The psalmist put it like this:

All creatures look to you
    to give them their food at the proper time.
When you give it to them,
    they gather it up;
when you open your hand,
    they are satisfied with good things.
When you hide your face,
    they are terrified;
when you take away their breath [*ruach*],
    they die and return to the dust.
When you send your Spirit [*ruach*],
    they are created,
    and you renew the face of the ground.[13]

There is a reason the Nicene Creed opens its stanza on the Holy Spirit by saying,

We believe in the Holy Spirit,
The Lord, the Giver of Life,
Who proceeds from the Father [and the Son],[14]
Who with the Father and the Son is worshiped and glorified.

The Spirit is God's Life within Godself, God's Life poured out *beyond* Godself onto and into us, making us alive.

THE GREAT RENEWAL

Which is why when the prophets of Israel spoke of the great renewal to come in the last days, the *ruach* of God was routinely bound up with their prophecies. The Lord said to Ezekiel,

This is what the Sovereign LORD says to these bones
[the dead-in-exile house of Israel]: I will make breath
[*ruach*] enter you, and you will come to life. I will
attach tendons to you and make flesh come upon you
and cover you with skin; I will put breath [*ruach*] in
you, and you will come to life. Then you will know
that I am the LORD.[15]

The *ruach* enters them, the bones subsequently rise up like a
"vast army,"[16] and once again Israel has life, hope, and a future.
Why? *Because they were breathed into by the* ruach *of God.* This
is the reason why there is a close association between the Spirit
of God and the resurrection of Jesus from the dead in the New
Testament. Listen to Paul:

And if the Spirit of him who raised Jesus from the dead
is living in you, he who raised Christ from the dead will
also give life to your mortal bodies because of his Spirit
who lives in you.[17]

Or as Peter puts it,

Christ also suffered once for sins, the righteous for the
unrighteous, to bring you to God. He was put to death
in the body but made alive in the Spirit.[18]

The early believers understood that Jesus of Nazareth, who
took our flesh and died our death, was rescued from the power
of the grave by none other than God the Father through the
agency of the Holy Spirit. Jesus is, in one sense, the very first

member of the house of Israel—the first member of the new humanity—to rise up out of the valley of dry bones, alive and indestructible.

And what is more, *the gift of his Spirit to us makes us participants in his resurrection life!* This is literally what the entire book of Acts is all about. The Holy Spirit, who was poured out on those early believers at the Day of Pentecost (Acts 2), was poured out *continually* on them throughout the rest of Acts, with the result that they exploded on the ancient Mediterranean world like a Kingdom-of-God-kind-of-party of life, hope, joy, and peace—the ministry of Jesus carried on through their Spirit-filled, Spirit-engulfed, Spirit-inspired lives and witnesses.

To know God the Holy Spirit is to be immersed in the unbreakable, world-creating, life-transforming Life of God. It is to find yourself yanked out of *your* grave, taking your first feeble steps into eternity. It is to have your humanity transfigured by the glory of the Kingdom. It is, as the writer of Hebrews puts it, to be "enlightened," to "tast[e] the heavenly gift," to feast on "the goodness of the word of God," and to know "the powers of the coming age"[19] as we await the glorious appearing of Christ Jesus at the consummation of the ages, the end of history, where death will be fully and finally overthrown, swallowed up in life.

It is to begin to live the resurrection, now.

(NEGLECTING) THE GIFT

Now you can see why it is such a tragedy when we neglect the person and presence of the Holy Spirit. We're not neglecting a "take it or leave it" aspect of the faith. We're neglecting the very means by which the living God communicates his life and grace to us. Without meaning to, we're saying no to the gift of God—the Gift that simply *is* the Holy Spirit, who is none other than God's gift of *himself* to us, the Gift by which we are drawn into union with the Giver.

Do you realize that *none* of the good things that God wants to give you come *except* by way of the Holy Spirit? The New Testament bears abundant witness to this. To point to one example, Paul says that no one is able to say "Jesus is Lord" unless the Holy Spirit makes it possible.[20] Just think about that—you can't do what we talked about in the last chapter except that the Spirit enables it. Similarly, Paul also says that our capacity to take the *"Abba,* Father" cry on our lips happens because of the Spirit crying out in us.[21] There again—you can't enter into the experience of God's fatherhood (which we discussed in chapter 1) except that the Spirit enables it.

St. Augustine's conversion—though not often thought of in this way—is one of my favorite examples of a life-giving, life-changing encounter with the Holy Spirit. Opening his spiritual autobiography entitled *Confessions* with the famous words "Our hearts are restless until they rest in You,"[22] Augustine goes on to describe his former life outside of Christ—a desperate and weary search for truth—saying,

> I have learnt to love you late, Beauty at once so ancient
> and so new! I have learnt to love you late! You were
> within me, and I was in the world outside myself.
> I searched for you outside myself and, disfigured as
> I was, I fell upon the lovely things of your creation.
> You were with me, but I was not with you.

Augustine sought pleasure, happiness, and meaning in the created things of God, but not in the Creator God himself, the Source from whom all blessing and goodness come. And then the moment happened that changed everything for Augustine, as it does for all who encounter God the Holy Spirit:

> You called me; you cried aloud to me; you broke my barrier of deafness. You shone upon me; your radiance enveloped me; you put my blindness to flight. You shed your fragrance about me; I drew breath and now I gasp for your sweet odour. I tasted you, and now I hunger and thirst for you. You touched me, and I am inflamed with love of your peace.[23]

It is the Spirit who makes the whole of our life in the Kingdom possible. The Spirit awakens our seeking and our searching after truth, and provokes our abandonment and our adoration of the Truth-in-Person, Jesus the Lord. It is the Spirit who leads us out of dead-end waywardness and onto the highway of salvation. It is the Spirit who communicates the grace of God to us, breaking our barriers of deafness, shining heaven's light on us, shedding the fragrance of God over us. It is the Spirit who is the very bond of our union with God, who makes us hunger and thirst for God and then satisfies us with the gift of God's own presence. It is the Spirit who works the Christ-life into us and causes us to bear fruit—love, joy, peace, forbearance (patience), kindness, goodness, faithfulness, gentleness, and self-control—for the Kingdom of God.[24]

All of this is the gift of the Spirit of God to all who would receive—which is what Peter says to the onlookers at Pentecost:

FILLED WITH THE SPIRIT

Repent and be baptized, every one of you, in the name
of Jesus Christ for the forgiveness of your sins. And you
will receive the gift of the Holy Spirit. The promise is
for you and your children and for all who are far off.[25]

The Spirit is for us. All of us. And for our children. And for
all who are far off. Wherever the Spirit blows, there is life.

Which is why we must welcome the Holy Spirit into our
lives every single chance we get. My porch time in the morning
is dedicated space where I welcome the life-giving, liberating,
eye-opening, fruit-creating work of the Holy Spirit.

But it doesn't stop there. I do it constantly. The apostle Paul
called the believers in Thessalonica to "pray without ceasing."[26]
That's what I do. Or try to do, anyway. Multiple times throughout the day I'll stop and pray, "Come, Holy Spirit." When I'm
vexed, troubled, and confused, I pray, "Come, Holy Spirit."
When I'm hopeful and eager and full of joy, I pray, "Come,
Holy Spirit." When I'm tired and worn out and feel like I just
can't take any more, I pray, "Come, Holy Spirit."

And I wait . . .

SURPRISED BY THE SPIRIT

And somehow or another, the Spirit comes. One of the things I
have learned and am learning is that when I pray, "Come, Holy
Spirit," I cannot pray it while secretly meaning, "Come the way
I *want* you to come." I must pray it saying, "Come the way I
need you to come—which you know better than I do."

That genuine openness, that willingness to be surprised, is
really the critical element in our engagement with the Holy

Spirit. When the Spirit descends, I have found, sometimes the descent is a subtle and barely perceptible sweetness. Sometimes it is a new sense of the love of God for me that refreshes my weary soul. Sometimes it is a strengthening of my sense of devotion to Jesus. Often it is an "agitation" of the waters of my life, reminding me that there is a relationship I need to make right, or prompting me to works of mercy for one of my neighbors.

And, of course, here and there it is something like what is described in Acts 2, "a sound like the blowing of a violent wind,"[27] where the Spirit crashes in, disturbing everything, awakening me in altogether unexpected ways to the Kingdom.

This daily, moment-by-moment welcome of the Holy Spirit is responsible, by the way, for the last two thousand years of church history. Across vastly different cultures and geographies, and despite stiff opposition, the gospel has advanced, and the church has grown. Why? Because the Spirit has been powerfully at work yanking men, women, and children out of their graves, quenching their every thirst with the Water of Life, baptizing them in holy fire, transforming their lives, uniting them with God and with one another, and making them together witnesses for the Kingdom.

That is the Spirit's work. And when you look at it this way, you'll understand that Pentecost was not an isolated incident destined to recede into the oblivion of history, evanescing as embattled saints trudge wearily to the Kingdom, but rather was *the initial combustion that set off a chain reaction that will one day engulf the cosmos in the flame of the Spirit.*

Make no mistake: We are living in an ever-intensifying Pentecost. The Lord Jesus said that when God gives the Spirit, he gives "without limit,"[28] meaning that what began in Acts 2 will grow in potency until the consummation of the ages. You and I are not living in some kind of desperate twilight, counting down the days till our rescue from a God-forsaken world. Instead, we are living in the rush of the *ruach* of God that, even now, is agitating every watery abyss of our lives, animating our families, communities, churches, and cities with the unbreakable life of the triune God, breathing into dry bones, making them rise and walk.

And so we lift up our voices—now in this way, now in that; in hearty praise and in quiet, adoring supplication—to the *ruach* of God who agitates and enlivens whatever he turns toward.

We trust that as the Spirit comes, in whatever manner and intensity, he'll come much as Augustine experienced: calling, crying, breaking through barriers, shining light, shedding heaven's fragrance on us, putting breath in our lungs, satisfying our desires and yet simultaneously making us hunger and thirst all the more for God, inflaming us with love for his peace.

And so we pray: "Come, Holy Spirit . . ."

. . . and wait . . .

FOR REFLECTION

What would it look like for you to open your life more to the gift of God the Holy Spirit?

PRAYER

> *Spirit of the Living God,*
> *Lord and Life-Giver,*
> *Hovering over the waters of my life,*

Come and agitate;
come and stir;
come and bring life.
I repent for all the ways I've held you at arm's length.
Enliven me in ways I did not know were possible.
Amen.

PART 2

PASSING THROUGH FIRE

*The spiritual life advances most profoundly through "crises"
that occur at each level of our relationship with the triune God:
when the experience of the Spirit is not ecstasy but agony;
when the leading of the Lord Jesus takes us to places we
did not expect and do not understand; and
when the face of the Father who loves us is
shrouded in darkness.*

*As we enter this three-dimensional struggle
with the triune God, we find:
purer love;
sturdier hope;
and deeper faith.*

THE PURIFYING FIRE

He will baptize you with the Holy Spirit and fire.

LUKE 3:16

[The] fire . . . burns as long as it has fuel.

ST. GREGORY OF NYSSA, *On the Soul and the Resurrection*

In the introduction to this book, I made mention of Abba Lot, who asked his friend Abba Joseph what else, beyond the daily habits of his devotional life, he could do to experience God. In response, Abba Joseph "stood up and stretched his hands towards heaven. . . . His fingers became like ten lamps of fire," and he said to Abba Lot, *"If you will, you can become all flame."*[1]

Stories like this are intended to be, in a sense, *iconic*. They are microcosms of deep reality, awakening in us holy desire, summoning us into the truths of which they speak.

The story of Lot and Joseph highlights a basic but critical aspect of the experience of God—namely, that whatever is at stake in our relationship with God is *more* than what we might call mere "religiosity," "spirituality," or even "morality." Lot tells Joseph that he is basically a good and faithful man. He says his office, he fasts a little, he prays and meditates, he lives peaceably with others, and he monitors his thought life honorably. What more is there?

A great deal more, as it turns out. If he is willing, he can become aflame with God—one in spirit with God, *full* of God's Holy Spirit, conformed to the image of Christ Jesus, drawn into the Kingdom—a radiant icon of what God intends for every human life.

We *can* be aflame with the love and goodness of God. We *can* be holy as he is holy.

But how does that happen?

"ON FIRE" FOR GOD?

Here we should pause. It is easy, frankly, to sentimentalize the idea of being aflame with God, and, in so doing, misunderstand what is at stake in the process. We idealize certain activities or religious states of being and then—having ticked the right behavioral or emotional boxes—believe that we have been set aflame by the Spirit. But have we?

Many people equate the "fire" of the Spirit with certain activities like Bible reading, prayer, and evangelism, or states of being like emotional ecstasy. When I was in high school, I was part of a small group of friends who were like this. We read our Bibles eagerly and talked often about what we were learning. We gathered for prayer and worship frequently. Spiritual activities, spiritual conversations, and spiritual experiences were our stock-in-trade. Often, the Lord would meet us powerfully, giving us "holy ground" moments far beyond our deserving. They marked all of us.

The problem was, tucked into those experiences were subtle hints of spiritual pride. Many of us looked down on those who didn't share our passion (I know I did). And folks who weren't interested in our message, many of us felt, simply weren't worth our time. The cancer of spiritual elitism was at work in us.

Now, had we been touched by the Spirit? Sure. I don't doubt that for a second. *But had we arrived?* Were we "all flame," as Abba Joseph describes? No. Not on your life. The Flame had just begun to descend, and there was burning yet to come. Speaking from my own experience, I can attest—almost none of it has been simple or painless.

Luke records that when John the Baptist appeared, preparing the people for the coming of the Messiah, he

said to the crowds coming out to be baptized by him, "You brood of vipers! Who warned you to flee from the coming wrath? Produce fruit in keeping with repentance. And do not begin to say to yourselves, 'We have Abraham as our father.' For I tell you that out of these stones God can raise up children for Abraham. The ax is already at the root of the trees, and every tree that does not produce good fruit will be cut down and thrown into the fire." [2]

Wrath. Fire. That's pleasant preaching for you. But here's what you have to understand: John is preaching out of a rich Old Testament imagination, where fire stood as a symbol for God and his work. On the one hand, fire figures in the Old Testament as one of the commonest metaphors for the judgment of God that sweeps evil away, cleansing, restoring, and transforming God's good world. The psalmist said, "Our God comes and will not be silent; a fire devours before him, and around him a tempest rages."[3]

But where does this fire issue from? Surprisingly it comes "from Zion," which is "perfect in beauty"—this mount of beautiful tranquility is the place from which "God shines forth"[4] with the purifying fire of judgment. Zion's perfection, the psalmist says, will descend *into* the corruption of society, beautifying it by judging and removing evil.

On the other hand, "fire" in the Old Testament is *also* a metaphor to describe the *person of Yahweh himself.* The Lord appeared to Abraham in Genesis as a smoking firepot,[5] to Moses as a burning bush,[6] and to the entire people of Israel as a cloud by day and a pillar of fire by night,[7] prompting Moses to describe Israel's God simply as "a consuming fire."[8] In the Old Testament imagination, therefore, when God "judges" us, he is not doing something *other than being what he is*—in proximity to us. The fire and the Person are one and the same, so that when we come into deep contact with the Person, we will inevitably experience him as fire. There is no other way.

John the Baptist understood this. And so he went on to say,

> I baptize you with water. But one who is more powerful
> than I will come, the straps of whose sandals I am not
> worthy to untie. He will baptize you with the Holy
> Spirit and fire.[9]

Jesus, John says, will immerse us in the Holy Spirit and *fire.* This is not the awakening of new religious sentiment in us (although it will certainly give rise to new feelings). Nor is it the inspiration to go and be a bit "nicer" in our daily lives (although this encounter will certainly produce good fruit for the world to feast on).

No, at its core, this is about the destruction of everything in us that stands against God. One of the most beautiful and challenging ideas in Christian theology is that the person of the Holy Spirit *is in fact* the bond of love that unites the Father and the Son. Which means that to experience God the Holy Spirit is to feel the heat of *that*. It is to feel the heat of *love*—God's love, an utterly unselfish love, a self-giving, others-preferring love, a love ever ready to transcend itself to the point of suffering for the good of the other. The Spirit, who is the *agape love* of the triune God, draws near with the fire that he is and has.

When *that* kind of love approaches, by its nature it burns defective love to the ground, killing as it brings to life, unmaking as it remakes. The God who is a consuming fire and a jealous God intends to draw us by his Holy Spirit into the burning heat of the triune life, changing us as we submit to his work.

EXPERIENCING THE PURIFYING FIRE

Failing to understand this, we will miss the better part of the Spirit's work in our lives, having falsely identified it only with gooey, positive "feelings," spikes in religious enthusiasm and action, or ecstatic spiritual experiences. There is a purging, purifying work of the Spirit that hurts like hell as it drags us into the heavens.

I know this because I have walked through it, and as a pastor, counselor, and friend, I have walked with many others who have similarly been touched by the purifying fire of the Spirit. It is frankly unpleasant, and it can take many forms.

Most simply and most commonly, we experience the purifying fire of the Spirit as the "burning" of conviction in prayer and worship. I cannot tell you how many times I've been lost in worship or private adoration of the Lord, when suddenly my attention is directed by the Spirit to someone I have mistreated, some errant pattern of thought, or some cherished offense or bit of self-righteousness that must be repented of. Unpleasant as it is, in the burning of conviction I am being baptized in the Holy Spirit, if I have eyes to see it. God the Holy Spirit comes to us often as the gentle agony of conviction.

Other times, we experience the purifying fire in our relationships with others, as we are confronted not with who we *believe ourselves* to be, but who we *really are* in community. Here, the agony we experience is our pride being shattered against the hard rock of truth. The confrontation is an immersion in the Holy Spirit, if we have eyes to see it.

GOD NEVER WASTES PAIN

But there is another place where we are touched by the purifying fire of the Spirit. I want to tread with care, but it needs to be said so that these places—and there are many of them—can be claimed for all that God intends them to be. Time and again I have seen and experienced the fire of the Spirit touching people's lives—my own and others'—through circumstances that we would rather not have walked through. Unpleasant as they are, God uses them to fill us with and shape us for his glory. We are baptized in the Spirit and fire.

The power of this was brought home to me years ago when I made acquaintance with a man who had once been a pastor. I shared a bit of my story, and then he started with his—a gut-wrenching tale of planting a church and watching it rise in health and influence only to spin wildly out of control and finally close its doors because of sin that he had nothing to do with. Within a matter of weeks, this precious congregation—and all my new friend's hopes and dreams for it—went from several hundred members to a mere memory. The personal losses he experienced in it were incalculable—his church, his ministry, his platform, to say nothing of the loss of many relationships. It remains one of the most painful stories I have ever heard.

I sat there that day speechless, heartbroken for him, when he concluded it with words I will never forget. "Andrew," he said to me, "I don't believe for a second that that was the perfect will of God for my life, or for my church."

"No," I said, "it was certainly not."

"And yet," he said to me, "I wouldn't trade that experience for anything in the world. What God did in me through it, who he made me to be, how he changed me . . . I could never give that up."

And then this: "What I know now that I didn't know before is that *God never wastes pain.*"

I have heard versions of that story perhaps hundreds of times in my life. People who walked through excruciating trials and found, much to their astonishment, that as they turned their faces to the Lord within the circumstance, they were changed. They had touched the sacred Fire of the Spirit behind the fire of their lives, the Fire that sits in, with, and under the many little fires that burn in and around us. And they were better for it. And because they were better for it, the world, in turn, was blessed by it. Zion's beauty broke forth in fire. So it is with God.

I am telling you—God the Holy Spirit is working in us through the many agonies we suffer. There is blessing in the breaking, if we'll recognize and receive it. We will be cleansed, purified, made useful to God for every good work.[10] One of Jesus' closest friends, Peter, put it memorably in a circular letter he wrote to the churches of Asia Minor, many of whom were suffering severe persecution and difficulty because of their faith. He wrote,

> In all this you greatly rejoice, though now for a little
> while you may have had to suffer grief in all kinds of
> trials. These have come so that the proven genuineness
> of your faith—of greater worth than gold, which
> perishes even though refined by fire—may result in
> praise, glory and honor when Jesus Christ is revealed.[11]

He likens the grief suffered in trials to the fire that melts gold in order to purify it. In the process, the dross of impurity is taken away, and for a time, the gold even loses its shape. But this is so—let it be noted—that the gold's luster may shine forth all the more, taking a shape useful to the one so shaping it. Brighter gold. Better shape. Lovelier form.

He will baptize you with the Holy Spirit and with fire . . .

AS LONG AS IT HAS FUEL

The metaphor of fire is common among the spiritual masters. Indeed, ever-greater union with God has often been understood to be accompanied by *purification and illumination.* But that process is by no means linear. There is no straightforward progression from one to the next. They are, in fact, different ways of talking about one and the same journey—the journey of surrendering to the Spirit's total work. We are purified and illuminated as we are drawn into union with God . . . we are brought into union as we are illuminated and purified . . . we are illuminated as we are purified and made one with the Lover of our souls.

Part of what this means is that the Love that has loved us from before the foundation of the earth will feel like scorching heat until all that stands against God in us has been burned away. Teresa of Avila likened the triumph of the love of God in the human heart to the way fire melts wax—surely a painful process for the wax! But the soul in that state, she says, is "prepared for the impress" of God's nature.[12] We begin to look more like God as we surrender to this "melting," "impressing" work.

One of the profoundest thinkers of the church, Gregory of Nyssa, made this a central piece of his spiritual theology. In a little treatise called *On the Soul and the Resurrection*, Gregory taught that purification and union with God are two sides of the same coin. The soul is initially drawn by the beauty of God, but as it begins the movement toward him in the "ecstasy" of spiritual desire, it experiences pain wrapped up in pleasure. And why is that? Because in the process of spiritual awakening, God is simultaneously rescuing the soul from the evils in which it is mired— like dragging someone out of a collapsed and burning building. To the soul being so rescued, the process feels like "wrath." The soul may wonder if God is angry with it. But Gregory assures us,

It is not out of hatred or vengeance for an evil life (in my opinion) that God brings painful conditions upon

sinners, when He seeks after and draws to Himself
whatever has come to birth for His sake; but for a
better purpose He draws the soul to Himself, who is
the fountain of all blessedness.[13]

It is God's *love* that burns the dross of evil out of the soul
as it draws it into the eternal blessedness of divine friendship.
And how long must that fire burn? Gregory answers, "As long
as it has fuel."[14] Ouch.

God, by the power of his Holy Spirit, will strip us of our
idols, burn away sin, and break our attachments to lesser things,
in order to reshape our wayward love so that it finally rises into
the Love that he is. The experience of the Spirit that initially
came as ecstasy gives way to what is oftentimes an agony. But
we must recognize this: That burning fire of the Spirit is nothing but the advent of the *love* of God into our lives, and we will
experience that burning heat as *pain* just as long as there is any
bit of us that is not fully surrendered to God.

THE MEGAPHONE

You and I need to learn to recognize the invitation of the Spirit
when it feels as though our lives are on fire. If we have eyes to
see it, we will discern God's adoring love in our agony, reaching
out to us to perfect us. It is a terrible honor he pays us, loving
us the way he does. C. S. Lewis wrote,

You asked for a loving God: you have one. The great
spirit you so lightly invoked, the "lord of terrible aspect,"
is present: not a senile benevolence that drowsily wishes

you to be happy in your own way . . . but the consuming fire Himself, the Love that made the worlds, persistent as the artist's love for his work and despotic as a man's love for a dog, provident and venerable as a father's love for a child, jealous, inexorable, exacting as love between the sexes. . . . It is certainly a burden of glory not only beyond our deserts but also, except in rare moments of grace, beyond our desiring.[15]

That fire, says Lewis, reaches to us most clearly and profoundly in the great and painful places of our lives. "God," he wrote, "whispers to us in our pleasures, speaks in our conscience, *but shouts in our pain: it is His megaphone to rouse a deaf world.*"[16]

The hard things that you and I walk through—it can be literally anything: the struggle with habitual sin; the loss of a job, of a relationship, of our health; the price we pay for standing for what is right in a world filled with injustice; the times when we feel desolate and alone and forsaken by God, or when the story of our lives takes a turn that we did not expect—all carry within them the potential for deeper transformation. Will we let the sting of circumstance lead us to greater surrender, greater yielding? Will we let pain lead us to penitence? Will we let the fire of adversity and hardship be a sacrament of the great Fire that is God?

The choice, truly, is ours. No one can or will make it for us. It belongs to us and us alone, and our futures—their everlasting blessedness or damnation—literally depend on it.

And, just to clear up any confusion, it is not a matter of ferreting out who precisely is responsible for the fires, who is to blame for the pain. Is the devil responsible? Are we responsible? Are others responsible? Is God responsible?

Such questions are often a strategy we employ to evade the ongoing invitation of the Spirit. Should we seek truth and justice in our situations? Of course we should. But we must also realize that the appropriate search for justice can easily distract us from the Spirit's work in us *through* the circumstance. Let us remember: God is not one "thing" among other "things" in the universe that we have to account for. According to the apostle Paul, God is the one in whom "we live and move and have our being."[17] That means, in part, that he is always present, working his will in, with, and under the movement and flow of history, subverting errant human wills, outpacing the enemy's diabolical stratagems, leading us to glory. The attempt to assign blame may not only block the possibility of our transformation; it tragically misses the larger story of God's activity in and around us.

Do you remember the story of Joseph in the book of Genesis? Subjected to massive pain and injustice, Joseph yielded himself to the Lord of his life, such that he could look back over all that had happened to him and say to those who had wronged him, "You *intended* to harm me, but God *intended* it for good to accomplish what is now being done, the saving of many lives."[18] The gracious divine intention saturated, overwhelmed, and finally subverted all evil human intention. Joseph's recognition of this allowed the conversation to transcend the logic of blame, lifting it up into the light of redemption, the logic of salvation. Yes, human beings did this, and it is not wrong to name that. But surely the more important questions are *What was God doing behind it? Who is God in the midst of it? Where is God taking us through it?*

CROSSING THE THRESHOLD

My friend Jack—a devoted husband, father, and grandfather, and a vibrant member of our church—was diagnosed with an incurable brain tumor. The news shocked the family. Up to that point in his life, Jack had been as strong as an ox and as tough as an old piece of leather. *How can this happen to Jack, of all people?* we wondered.

Up and down his health went, over the course of many months. Jack consistently defied the expectations of the doctors as he faced the prospect of his mortality with winsomeness, grace, and good humor. It was inspiring.

One day Jack and I caught up over coffee. "I'm curious," I said to him. "What has having to face your mortality done to you spiritually?"

His reply was instant: "Well, in the first place, I guess I don't really care what people think of me anymore."

I chuckled a bit. When you are standing at the very threshold of eternity, readying yourself to see the face of God, people's opinions—which most of us are very (foolishly and to our detriment) driven by—are suddenly a lot less important. Jack was experiencing the grace of what the ancients called "detachment"—a dying to our own egos and to the opinions of others as we increasingly come alive to God. It was clear that grace was powerfully at work in Jack.

He continued: "Secondly, and maybe this will sound weird to you, but while I don't care what people think *of* me, I do find that I care *for* people a great deal more than I used to." Agape love was displacing in Jack the irrational fear of what others thought. Again, it was obvious to me that Christlikeness was growing profoundly in him through the circumstance.

And then he concluded: "And lastly, God is more present to me than he has ever been. I sense him now more than ever. I see him everywhere."

Was the tumor "from God"? I don't believe that for a second. But remember—*God wastes nothing.* And, as Lewis said, in the great pains of our lives he shouts to us, inviting us into deeper life with him. The fire of the tumor became for Jack a sacrament of the great Fire that unmakes and purifies our souls as it takes us into God.

Part of what struck me so profoundly that day with Jack was that, in a sense, he was living the truth of what every Christian is called to live all the time. Jesus said that if we lost our lives, we would find them. That if we abandoned our whole existence to God, we'd touch the core of true life. In dying daily, the Scripture teaches, we live. And as we press deeper into this death to self, we begin to enter the place where Madame Guyon says "your will breaks free of you completely and becomes free to be joined to the will of God!" God's will lives and loves increasingly in us, and we live and love increasingly in God. In this place, "you will desire only what He desires."[19] The Holy Spirit will burn us down to "yes"—and there we will be aflame with light and love, ready to bless the world in our abandonment to God. Jack's crisis had forced that on him. But in truth, it is the "crisis" that is to mark each one of us, at each moment of our lives—the crisis of surrender that becomes the threshold of new life and possibility and freedom.

And this is why we must learn to welcome the Spirit in the agonized places, for they carry within them the possibility of great transformation. John O'Donohue says that "everything that happens to you has the potential to deepen you."[20] He's right. That hand of God reaches to us in the concrete events of our lives, even and especially the difficult ones, calling us deeper.

And the reality is that there is a great deal that needs to be cut back, burned away, and refigured in us that we are simply not capable of doing on our own. If we could, we would have done it by now. But we couldn't. We can't. We need God's help. And that is precisely the gift of the hard things—God does for us and in us what we cannot.

Thomas Merton wrote, "In getting the best of our secret attachments—ones which we cannot see because they are principles of spiritual blindness—our own initiative is almost always useless. We need to leave the initiative in the hands of God working in our souls either directly in the night of aridity and suffering, or through events and other men."[21] In those places, he says, "when we seem to be destroyed and devoured, it is then that the deep and secret selfishness that is too close for us to identify is stripped away from our souls."[22] The Fire behind the fires scorches and heals us.

The period following our departure from Denver represented just one of those seasons for me. I loved who I was and what I did in Denver. I wanted to do it forever. And when I finally had to let it all go, I wept. It felt to me like a comprehensive, existential loss—of identity, meaning, relationships, work, and an imagined future. *Who am I without this?* I often thought. *What am I supposed to do? What does any of this even mean?*

For a long time after our move to Colorado Springs, I would head out in the mornings to my front porch to pray, and just sit in God's presence, stupefied. *How did we wind up here? Who is to blame?* I would turn what felt to me like an untimely ending to my ministry in Denver over and over in my mind, lifting up to the Lord questions for which there were no answers. Just the gift of his presence and the promise that somehow, through it, he was saving me, and the world around me.

Over time, a funny thing started happening to me. I discovered that in that place of stupefaction, a new tenderness, a new openness, a new flexibility began to steal into my being. I was able to look back on my time in Denver and see that for all its beauty and meaning, there were also great compulsions, rigidities, and fears that drove me, and they needed to die. Being called to lay that ministry down was a severe mercy. Severe because it hurt in a way I cannot describe. Mercy because it delivered me from a great deal of madness, leading me deeper into the sane, sound, burning love of God. As much as it hurt, it was an authentic, deep experience of the Spirit. The Fire behind the fires.

Will you receive the gifts that the Lord, by his Spirit, is trying to give you in the hard places? Merton said it best when he wrote,

> Every moment and every event of every man's life on earth plants something in his soul. For just as the wind carries thousands of winged seeds, so each moment brings with it germs of spiritual vitality that come to rest imperceptibly in the minds and wills of men. Most of these unnumbered seeds perish and are lost, because men are not prepared to receive them. . . .

We must learn to realize that the love of God
seeks us in every situation, and seeks our good. His
inscrutable love seeks our awakening. True, since this
awakening implies a kind of death to our exterior self,
we will dread His coming in proportion as we are
identified with this exterior self and attached to it.[23]

The fire of God's love is ever approaching, and we will dread
its coming in proportion to our attachment to lesser things.
Will you respond? Will I? Will we receive the gift of the Gift
tucked into every event of our lives? Will we be transformed by
the Fire that burns in the fires of our agony?

Or will we cling to life as we know it, to our "selves" as we
know them to be, tragically missing the Spirit's work?

The choice is ours.

FOR REFLECTION

What are some places in your life now that the Lord may want
to touch with the purifying fire of his Spirit?

PRAYER

Holy Spirit,
Fire of divine love,
Tempest of everlasting beauty,
Shine forth into my life.
Burn away all in me that opposes God.
Conquer me with and for the love of the triune God,
so that my life comes to resemble that of Christ Jesus.
Amen.

THE STORY WE DIDN'T EXPECT

[Jesus said,] "Get behind me, Satan! You are a stumbling block to me;
you do not have in mind the concerns of God,
but merely human concerns."

MATTHEW 16:23

Jesus has a different vision of maturity: It is the ability and
willingness to be led where you would rather not go.

HENRI NOUWEN, In the Name of Jesus

One of the most dramatic and gripping scenes in the Gospels occurs toward the end of the life of Jesus. Matthew, Mark, and Luke each record a version of it. The Last Supper is complete, Judas the Betrayer has departed from the company of the twelve disciples in order to hand Jesus over to the Jewish ruling authorities, and Jesus, knowing that the hour of his death is nearly upon him, heads out into the night with the eleven to pray. Luke takes us into the action:

> Jesus went out as usual to the Mount of Olives, and his disciples followed him. On reaching the place, he said to them, "Pray that you will not fall into temptation." He withdrew about a stone's throw beyond them, knelt down and prayed, "Father, if you are willing, take this cup from me; yet not my will, but yours be done." [1]

The story captures our imaginations in part because of Luke's powerful depiction of Jesus' manifest agony as he looked toward his coming hour. "And being in anguish," continues Luke, "he prayed more earnestly, and his sweat was like drops of blood falling to the ground."[2]

Like drops of blood. Have you ever prayed like that? With clenched teeth and white knuckles and sweat rolling in beads down your forehead? Jesus did. The detail alerts us to a truth that much sentimental piety often forgets—namely, that the one with whom we deal, the Lord Jesus Christ, was, for all his divinity, *incarnate* of the Holy Spirit *and the virgin Mary* and therefore *truly human*, as the creed declares. Like us, he agonized. Like us, he suffered anguish. Like us, he wrestled with the divine will—God the Only Begotten, incarnate for us and for our salvation, wrestling with God. Imagine that. Divinity did not overpower humanity. Rather, it sat within it, honored it, and radiated through it.

And that is perhaps the thing that captures us most about the scene—at least it does so for me—that the anguish notwithstanding, Jesus surrenders himself to the will of the Father, to a story that he admits he would not have chosen for himself. Shocking as it may be to our ears, the Son of God begs for any path other than the one laid out before him: "Father, if you are willing," he says, "take this cup from me." Luke has the request qualified by an "if"—*if you are willing*. Mark's version of the scene, however, puts it even more bluntly: "*Abba*, Father," Jesus said, to the one whose face and favor he had known from all eternity, "everything is possible for you." Indeed. Therefore, he pleads with his Abba: "*Take this cup from me.*"[3]

No qualifiers. Just a plea to startle our religious ears. *I don't want to do this*, the Son of God said, bold-faced, to his Father in heaven. *Take the cup.*

The road had narrowed to this one point, and for Jesus there were no longer—if ever there had been—"options." There was only this: Walk the appointed path, or do the unthinkable and step into the abyss of disobedience.

And there, with the whole story of our salvation hanging precariously in the balance, the man Jesus, who is God, finally yields: *Yet not my will, but yours be done.* He lives the truth of the prayer he taught to the very end: *Thy kingdom come, thy will be done, on earth as it is in heaven.* Even—especially—when the divine "thy will" and the human "my will" come into conflict, Jesus yields, and so begins the march of courageous passion that will lead to our salvation, when the Son of God declares from the cross, "It is finished."[4]

MASTERS OF OUR FATES, CAPTAINS OF OUR SOULS

At some point, each one of us, if we are serious about following Jesus, will face moments that have the character of Gethsemane, where what we want, what we expect and hope for our stories— the stories we have come to know and love in following Jesus— comes into conflict with the will of the God who calls us into *his* story. And we will have to choose, when the story that we didn't expect and perhaps didn't *want* is thrust on us—will it be his will, or ours? Will we yield?

No one does it easily. It's not in our nature. Martin Luther taught that since the Fall, the human will is (in Latin) *"incurvatus in se"*[5]—turned in on itself, bent inward, so that what we "naturally" will is *ourselves*: what *we* want, what *we* desire, what *we* think is good. *We* want to call the shots, and the last thing we want is having our comfortable, self-made realities impinged on by someone *else's* will. The thought is noxious to us.

In my judgment, modern society is the *incurvatus* will writ large. It is so much a part of the fabric of who we are that we have a hard time noticing it. Want proof? Read the lines of this poem, and see if they don't stir something in you:

> *Out of the night that covers me,*
>   *Black as the pit from pole to pole,*
> *I thank whatever gods may be*
>   *For my unconquerable soul.*
>
> *In the fell clutch of circumstance*
>   *I have not winced nor cried aloud.*
> *Under the bludgeonings of chance*
>   *My head is bloody, but unbowed.*
>
> *Beyond this place of wrath and tears*
>   *Looms but the Horror of the shade,*
> *And yet the menace of the years*
>   *Finds and shall find me unafraid.*
>
> *It matters not how strait the gate,*
>   *How charged with punishments the scroll,*
> *I am the master of my fate,*
>   *I am the captain of my soul.*[6]

The poem is "Invictus" by the nineteenth-century Englishman William Ernest Henley. While recovering from an emergency surgical procedure to save his right leg (his left leg had been amputated at the knee after a bout with tuberculosis when he was a teenager), Henley penned these words. *Invictus* is a Latin word that means "unconquered," and the poem was Henley's courageous defiance in the face of his circumstance. "You may take my limbs, but you will not take my soul," says the poet. Why? Because "I am the master of my fate," and "I am the captain of my soul."

The poem stirs us. It stirs me. But should it? How do we assess it from a Christian standpoint?

THE WILLING WILL

There is a sense in which Henley's defiant claims are true. Part of the glory and dignity of being human, according to Christianity, is that we have been given the gift of choice—who we will be and what we will do with ourselves. Out of his own boundless freedom, God has granted his image-bearers a measure and portion of their own.

But Christianity does not stop there, by simply recognizing our freedom. What it asserts is that in order to flourish, we must learn to yield our freedom to the will of God. The human will must match up with the divine will. Freedom, choice, is *for* something. To the biblical mind, the value of any choice is measured by the end for which the choice was made in the first place—God—and not by the mere fact that choice exists.

According to the record of Genesis, our first parents, Adam and Eve, were not just given *freedom*; they were given *commands*. "Be fruitful and increase in number," says the Lord to our forebears; "fill the earth and subdue it. Rule over the fish in the sea and the birds in the sky and over every living creature that moves on the ground."⁷ Adam and Eve would thrive as their wills joined hands with the will of the Creator. Their freedom was to be oriented toward something, toward someone—toward God and his good pleasure, his will. The will of God is the counterpart and perfection of human freedom, and it includes *positive commands* like "Fill the earth," *permissions* like "You are free to eat from any tree in the garden,"⁸ and also *negative commands*, or *prohibitions*: "You must not eat from the tree of the knowledge of good and evil, for when you eat from it you will certainly die."⁹

The message is clear: To step out of God's will is to step into destruction. The human will can tragically annihilate itself. By the same token—buckle up for a second—the only way for the will to be saved is *for the will to learn to will the will of the one who made it and loves it.*

When it *wills* a good—The Good—beyond itself.

When we learn to pray with Jesus in Gethsemane, "Not my will, but yours be done."

I realize that was a bit esoteric, but most of us, I believe, understand intuitively what I am talking about. If you've ever walked with a loved one through addiction, you know the dynamic: The addict starts out with a choice, but as their engagement with self-destructive behavior increases, the behavior shapes the will itself. Before long, the will *wills* the behavior in a way that becomes increasingly compulsive. It is, in other words, more and more difficult to choose otherwise. Before long, the will is sucked into a vortex of compulsivity and has become totally captive—sold into slavery. The only way out, truly, is an act of God, which is why most twelve-step programs acknowledge that there is no remedy outside of reliance on a "higher power." God needs to break through to rescue the *incurvatus* will.

FINDING OUR "SELVES"

In order to live, the will must die and be born again with and into a power beyond itself. Sound familiar? Jesus once said, "Everyone who sins is a slave to sin."[10] The self-guided will that wills only itself is, in fact, tragically captive. But, he continues, "If the Son sets you free, you will be free indeed."[11] Only Jesus can really liberate the will. Only Jesus can make us free. Elsewhere he says, "Anyone who loves their life will lose it, while anyone who hates their life in this world will keep it for eternal life."[12]

The message is clear: The way to save our freedom, paradoxically, is by giving it up. The way to save our lives is by losing them. The way to save our stories is by yielding them to another. We—the masters of our fates and the captains of our souls—can only really be so to the extent that we surrender our self-mastery, our self-captainship; to the extent, in other words, that we say yes to Jesus.

If you think about it, this is really the entire shape and structure of discipleship. Consider the rite of passage that has historically marked the new believer's entry into the church, as a member both of Christ and of his people—baptism. Paul writes of baptism using stark imagery:

> Or don't you know that all of us who were baptized
> into Christ Jesus were baptized into his death? We

were therefore buried with him through baptism into death in order that, just as Christ was raised from the dead through the glory of the Father, we too may live a new life.[13]

Paul is saying that in baptism our old way of being *dies with Christ.* To take the plunge, to enter the waters with Jesus, is to say no to our "selves." It is, to put it one way, a *funeral service.* "Here lies Andrew Arndt, buried with Christ, this _____ (*day in ordinals*) day of _____ (*month*), _____ (*year*)." And in that identification, a whole new way of being is made possible. Paul writes that "just as Christ was raised from the dead through the glory of the Father, we too may live a new life." Andrew Arndt is not destroyed, but is, rather, put to death and raised to life again—lifted up, elevated, and transformed by the encounter with the Lord. In the act of self-surrender, we become more our "selves" than we ever would have been on our own.

It's counterintuitive, I know—that we find ourselves not by going *inside* to determine who we "really" are but, rather, by going *outside* of ourselves to meet the Lord, who takes us and makes more of us than we ever could have made of ourselves. But it's the gospel. And it has marked followers of Jesus from the very first.

In discussing the apostle Peter's transforming journey with the Lord, theologian Hans Urs von Balthasar wrote,

Simon the fisherman could have explored every region of his ego prior to his encounter with Christ, but he would not have found "Peter" there; for the present, the "form" summed up in the name "Peter," the particular mission reserved for him alone, is hidden in the mystery of Christ's soul. . . . Each time Simon follows the understanding native to "Simon" he will go dangerously astray, whereas he will always hit the mark when, refusing to "confer with flesh and blood," he attends only to his commission, which reveals the Father's will to him.[14]

Just as we talked about in chapter 2, it's not until you really put your life in the hands of Jesus that you begin to *find* your life. "Simon" becomes "Peter" not by exerting his will in a grand act of self-actualization but by saying yes in all simplicity to Jesus. In losing his life as he knew it, he finds his life—a life that, in retrospect, wound up being so much greater and more significant than he ever could have created for himself. Simon the fisherman becomes Peter the apostle—a key leader in a movement that would sweep across the globe. That's what surrendering your life to Jesus does.

MAKE YOUR PLANS...

But here's the thing—you never really graduate from the call to self-surrender. Oh, I know, many people talk as if the call to surrender your life to Jesus is a one-off deal, something you do at the moment of your conversion. We sing choruses of "I Surrender All" as folks respond to the preacher's altar call, giving their lives to the Lord.[15] And that's good. We should do that. And we should remember that at that moment, for those folks, and also for us, *the surrender has only just begun.*
The dying to self that such a moment represents is not a

hurdle you leap over on the way *to* the Kingdom; it is the way *of* the Kingdom. Christ Jesus, whose whole life was one massive "offering" to the Father in the way of self-surrender, by the Spirit continually draws our lives into the eddy of that deep and costly obedience that culminates in the Cross.

It's taken me a long time to realize this. When I was in high school, I attended a prayer meeting in which the leader of the meeting walked over to me and said, "Andrew Arndt, I sense the Lord saying to you: 'Make your plans . . . and know that I will change them.'"

His words immediately grabbed my attention. I've wrestled with them a great deal. There are times that I've wondered, *Was he just being mean? Did he concoct a "word" from the Lord because he had it out for me? Was there some demonic impulse at work there to discourage me from taking initiative, from striking out boldly on my own? Should I just ditch the memory of those words altogether? Wouldn't I be more fulfilled?*

But the longer I've wrestled with them, the longer I've *lived*, the more I see that those words were indeed an authentic "word" from God for me, because they represent the cross-shaped path of every authentic follower of Christ. Following Jesus is not about exercising our creative wills in whatever way we think is best. It is, rather, discerning where and how we are being led, and then being willing to say yes to that—even and especially when that leading conflicts with what we wanted for our lives.

All of us will come to these moments. Once you choose to follow Jesus, they will happen again and again. And until the day of your death, they will only increase in intensity. You don't graduate from self-surrender. Ever. Just when you think you've gotten a handle on your story and what Jesus is doing with it, he'll up and change direction, and upon you will be thrust a story you did not expect. What do you do then? And what is God doing to you in it?

WHEN THE STORY TAKES A TURN

Simon Peter certainly experienced this. After leaving behind everything to follow Jesus, "Simon" becomes "Peter" in the new movement that explodes on ancient Palestine. He has a place and role in it. Whatever sense of loss he might have felt at leaving his old life behind is quickly eclipsed by the new purpose and identity he has come to know in following Jesus. Driving out demons, healing the sick, raising the dead, announcing the Kingdom—it's all pretty heady stuff.

What is more, Jesus has elevated Peter to a preeminent role among the Twelve. Frequently we see the trio of Peter, James, and John brought into the most private and intimate conversations and moments of encounter with Jesus. Jesus confides in them and leans on them to be *leaders among the leaders*. What must that have felt like for Simon Peter? Surely, he felt a great deal of responsibility and pride at being given this role. Jesus who gave it also recognizes and blesses it.

One such moment of blessing occurs at a pivotal juncture in the ministry of Jesus. At a place called Caesarea Philippi one day, Jesus asks the disciples, "Who do people say that I am?" The disciples offer Jesus reports on what they've heard folks say, so Jesus sharpens the question: "What about *you*? Who do *you* say that I am?" And Peter, always willing to go first, blurts out, "You are the Messiah, the Son of the Living God." Jesus validates Peter, saying,

> Blessed are you, Simon son of Jonah, for this was not
> revealed to you by flesh and blood, but by my Father
> in heaven. And I tell you that you are Peter, and on this
> rock I will build my church, and the gates of Hades will
> not overcome it. I will give you the keys of the kingdom
> of heaven; whatever you bind on earth will be bound in
> heaven, and whatever you loose on earth will be loosed
> in heaven.[16]

The Father, Jesus affirms, is at work in Peter's life—revealing to him the identity of the Messiah and therefore making him fit to lead an institution at which the very gates of hell will tremble.

Like I said—*heady stuff.* Can you imagine what this must have felt like to Peter? Place, identity, purpose, validation. Yes, leaving Dad's fishing business behind was tough. *But this is surely a promotion* . . . Peter is, for all intents and purposes, promised the chairmanship of the board among the Twelve, leading the leaders who will carry forward the Kingdom movement inaugurated in Jesus.

And then,

> Jesus began to explain to his disciples that he must go
> to Jerusalem and suffer many things at the hands of the
> elders, the chief priests and the teachers of the law, and
> that he must be killed and on the third day be raised
> to life.[17]

Wait, what? Out of nowhere, Jesus takes what must have seemed to the disciples a morbid turn. *Go to Jerusalem and suffer many things . . . ?* Why in the world would Jesus want to do that? The movement, for the most part, is working. Yes, there's been a bit of tension with the religious establishment, but with enough time and some savvy marketing, surely things can be smoothed over. Who knows? Maybe with enough time the new movement will simply overwhelm the old—a bloodless revolution.

The disciples had to have thought that this new direction from Jesus—"go to Jerusalem"—was incalculably foolish. And so Peter, newly minted as the now-and-future leader of the movement, takes a moment to try to stabilize his psychologically unstable friend:

Peter took him aside and began to rebuke him. "Never, Lord!" he said. "This shall never happen to you!" [18]

Like, really—how can you even think this way, Jesus? Yes, it's been a busy season and we've seen a little bit of adversity. But this movement *cannot* fail. It *won't* fail. We won't let it. And neither will God. So, stop already with all this dark, brooding talk. You're going to scare everyone.

And in response to Peter, Jesus takes the conversation to a new level:

Jesus turned and said to Peter, "Get behind me, Satan! You are a stumbling block to me; you do not have in mind the concerns of God, but merely human concerns." [19]

Jesus sees what is at work in Peter. It is nothing but that old demonic impulse to protect and enthrone the "self." Peter's thought lives at the level of the merely human. And to live at the level of the *merely* human—detached from divine obedience— is to live at the level of Satan, humanity's age-old adversary, who once and always tempts humanity to live independent of the will of God.

No, for Jesus, this movement of the story—toward Jerusalem, Gethsemane, and finally Golgotha—dark and incomprehensible as it may seem to the disciples, is appointed for him by the Father, who governs all things according to his good purpose. And there is more:

> Then Jesus said to his disciples, "Whoever wants to be my disciple must deny themselves and take up their cross and follow me. For whoever wants to save their life will lose it, but whoever loses their life for me will find it. What good will it be for someone to gain the whole world, yet forfeit their soul? Or what can anyone give in exchange for their soul? For the Son of Man is going to come in his Father's glory with his angels, and then he will reward each person according to what they have done."[20]

Because the disciples belong to the Son, who offers up his life to the will of the Father, *they also* will be called to offer up *their* lives to the Father through the Son. *They also* will have to enter this dark cloud of obedience, willing to suffer what feels like the annihilation of their stories for the sake of the greater Story of God. And in this they will find themselves, they will find *life*. As George MacDonald said,

We can live in no way but that in which Jesus lived, in which life was made in him. That way is, to give up our life. . . . Till then we are not alive. . . . The whole strife and labour and agony of the Son with every man, is to get him to die as he died. . . . When a man truly and perfectly says with Jesus, and as Jesus said it, "Thy will be done," he closes the everlasting life-circle; the life of the Father and the Son flows through him.[21]

The incomprehensible way of the cross is not just for Jesus; it is for all those who call him Lord. And every step on the way will therefore have something of the character of the cross— a *vestigium crucis*, as it were. We will be called to ever-deepening surrender through which our lives, offered to the Father through the Son, are made more meaningful than they ever would have been otherwise, lifted up into the light of eternity, transfigured with glory.

IN THE BOAT WITH JESUS

I have been a follower of Jesus all of my life, and do you know what I know for certain? That no one achieves significant spiritual maturity without passing through not one but *many* seasons when their story with Jesus as they knew it took a dark, incomprehensible, and unexpected turn. It is part of the path that is laid out for all of us.

The turn can and does take many forms. The loss of a job, the loss of a spouse, the breakdown of a relationship, a vocational crisis, a health crisis. It can be literally anything.

I know that many will object to this. "Are you saying that *God* took away the job, the spouse, the relationship, the health? Are you saying that *God* thrust this on me? Some of this is clearly the work of the devil."

I won't argue with you. Just like we talked about in the last chapter, some of these painful and unexpected situations are indeed the work of the devil; some are the work of fallen humans; and some—at the broadest level—are simply the by-product of living in a fallen and finite world.

But that's the thing—right here we are butting up against what Christians through the ages have called the mystery of divine Providence. That somehow, in ways that we cannot adequately explain, God uses the dark and incomprehensible both to make us into who he wants us to be and to subvert and finally overthrow the darkness and incomprehensibility of our world. In other words, our world is so riddled with the darkness of sin that *if God is to do anything in us and in our world*, he must, he *has to* work precisely through that darkness. There is no other way. Jacob's words, "Surely the LORD is in this place, and I was not aware of it," apply here as well. Remember—in all things and at all times, *it is God with whom we deal.*

Consider Christ Jesus himself. Was his suffering at the hands of wicked men an incomprehensible evil? Rome and Jerusalem—two of the most powerful political and religious institutions of the day—lynched an innocent man; indeed, the *best man who ever lived.* Never was a righteous sufferer more righteous and less guilty than Jesus. Never was an execution more heinous and ill-deserved—an unqualified evil.

And yet, at the same time, we need to ask ourselves (if we

hope to grasp something of the deep way that God works), wasn't it also the pivot point of the divine plan to conquer evil and renew all things? Indeed, it was. Both at the same time. The good will of God radiated through and finally subverted and swallowed up evil. One ancient Easter hymn of the church expresses this by saying that the work of God in Christ has resulted in a "trampling down [of] death by death."[22] Just take that in.

All of our stories—all their twists and turns and unexpected breakdowns—are tainted with sin. Christians are people who recognize that in, with, and under it all, God is at work—beautifying and perfecting us, and saving the world. Faith is that which trusts that God is present in it all, even when we can't see or understand, even when it makes no sense to our little minds. And that faith gives rise to great hope—that in and through the incomprehensible, we still and always have a future with God. And so we are safe to surrender control of our neat and orderly worlds into the hands of the God who made us and loves us and governs all things according to his purpose. There is great peace in so doing.

In the summer of 2016, when it felt like the ground was starting to shift under our feet with the church we pastored in Denver, I remember thinking, *This can't be happening, Lord. Not now. The church is finally healthy and thriving and vibrant. Now I ought to be settling in for the long haul. What in the world is going on? Am I just burned out?*

After a great deal of prayer and discernment with friends,

family, and mentors we trusted, we came to a place of clarity—
we were disoriented because *our plans* and *what God was doing*
had come into conflict. A summer sabbatical confirmed it.
When we came back to the community after several months
away, as glad as we were to see them and they to see us, it was
clear: *The church had been fine without us.* More than fine, it was
thriving. We knew that it was time to lay it down.

Now, if you're at all like me, you'll understand exactly what
I wanted to do next: *Call the elders, make an announcement,
and get the "show" of our transition on the road.* Why delay the
inevitable? But at the encouragement of those who had walked
with us in the journey of discernment, we sensed the Lord saying, "Don't make an announcement. Don't try to control this
process. Just go back to work. Watch, and wait."

So we did. It was excruciating. Days turned into weeks,
which turned into months, and I felt so *stupid*. *What in the
world is the point of all of this?* I wondered—often and aloud—to
the Lord.

Truth be told, I think that the "point" was and is much
larger and more incomprehensible than I will ever know. And
that, I believe, is in itself part of what God was doing in me
through it. He was disabusing me of the compulsive need to
know, to feel that I *had a grasp* on what he was doing. He was
teaching me—at the level of my vocation and calling, at the
level of my story—how to walk in the dark.

The experience of that season threw me into a depth of
knowing and being known by God I had never felt. The beloved
in the Song of Songs says, "His mouth is sweetness itself; he is
altogether lovely."[23] I began to experience that. Hanging on his
words, his incomprehensible activity, both focused and relaxed

me. My prayer life started to change. Instead of trying to crack open the mind of God to figure out his plans so that I could rush out and accomplish something for him, I would instead sit in my "prayer chair," coffee in hand, welcoming the Holy Spirit, and then just "watch" with my spiritual eyes . . . entering into that place of responsiveness to his will, his Word, my attention transfixed by his countenance.

The impact that began to have on my soul was remarkable. As I held that space, old anxieties started to melt. Old angers and fears began to evaporate. The fires of ungodly ambition began to die down, quenched by the cool water of the Spirit. "And the things of earth will grow strangely dim, / In the light of His glory and grace,"[24] the old song goes. It was something like that.

One morning late in the fall, I was on a retreat with our staff and leadership team up in the mountains, and I went for a walk to pray, holding the "waiting space" in my heart. As I walked and prayed, I sensed the Lord create an image for me, to help me understand the spiritual space he had led me into. The next day, I found a pen and my journal and wrote down what I saw and heard in my spirit. The image served (and, in many ways, continues to serve) as a North Star for me.

I saw myself in a boat with Jesus. It was a little wooden rowboat. I could hear the *clap, clap* of the waves on the side of the boat, feel the gentle rocking, and hear the creakiness of the wood as it bent and flexed.

Darkness was all around. I could not see anything outside of the boat; only inside. Mostly my attention was taken up with Jesus. My sense was that we were in a vast expanse. No shore for miles, although I couldn't be sure. Honestly, the shore could have been a dozen yards away, and I wouldn't have known it. It didn't matter. I was with Jesus, and I was enjoying it.

I couldn't exactly make out a rhyme or a reason to what he was doing. Here and there he would cast a line out one side and just sit. Other times he would grab the oars (he expressly forbade me from touching them) and row to some location that apparently was important for us to be, in what was all a dark void to my eyes. At other times, he would futz around with little odds and ends in the boat. And still, I would sit and watch him, enjoying the rocking, the slight creaking, and the clap, clap. Here and there he would break off what he was doing and just look at me with a knowing smile. My heart would fill up with peace and a profound contentment. Those eyes . . . that face . . .

At times, I would start wondering about things. So I would ask, "What about my family? Where are we going? What are you doing?" He would reply, "Are you enjoying this?" "Yes," I would answer. "Good. And do you trust me?" "Of course," I would say. "Wonderful. Then you may continue to do so." Instantly I would settle back in, lovingly watching his odd and incomprehensible activity, full-hearted.

And that was the strange thing about the image. There was no sense of movement per se. I didn't sense a "destination" in it.

There was no narrative for me to cling to. It was just him. Us. Together. And he—very much in charge. We were being blown along gently to God knows where and he was doing God knows what. And it was fine. I was happy.

I still am. The rocking. The creaking. The *clap, clap*. And that face. Those eyes. I just keep watching him . . . There is literally nothing else.

BEING LED

There is literally nothing else. That is, I think, one important way to think about discipleship. We fix our eyes on Jesus—not on our story, identity, calling, purpose, or any of that—and let him sort out the details, clinging to his every word, to his odd and incomprehensible activity.

Years have passed since that moment, but the spiritual space it created remains. I did, in perfect honesty, at first think that it was a seasonal thing. At some point, surely, the Lord would give light to the dark expanse and show me once more what it was all *really* about and where we were *really* going the whole time.

Now, don't get me wrong—the Lord has led and guided us to new places of vocational fruitfulness. The story continues. But that leading and guiding has not been *at the expense of* the intimacy and vocational un-knowing that came on me through that season. I don't, frankly, think that the Lord intends me ever to "graduate" from the simplicity of being willing to be *led*—even when it makes no sense. I am convinced that once he brings us there, he does not intend for any of us to. And why would we want to, anyway? In the end,

I think discipleship is always supposed to be like this—a place of peaceful attention as we hang on his face, his words, his activity, and nothing more.

Does it sound beautiful? It is. But make no mistake, if you walk this path, you will feel *odd*, for this way is dramatically out of step with the way of the world. The world conceives of maturity as a progressive expansion of our powers of self-actualization. *Become someone; do something; write your own story!*

Followers of Jesus are different. They do not see "self-actualization" as the way to the Kingdom. Followers of Jesus are people who in fact see "self-actualization" as the way to the kingdom of darkness. The Kingdom of light is a kingdom marked by the cross—by many crosses—of self-abandonment and self-emptying. Maturity in the Kingdom is not the exaltation of the *I*. Maturity in the Kingdom is the *I* becoming supple, like clay in the hands of the all-embracing "Thou" of the triune God, where we can say with Mary, the mother of Jesus, "Behold, the Lord's servant. May it be done to me according to your word."[25]

The great spiritual writer of the twentieth century, Henri Nouwen, describes the Christian leader of the future as a person who is willing to lead by "being led." Using the conversation between Peter and Jesus in John 21 as his cue (see John 21:18), Nouwen writes,

> The world says, "When you were young you were dependent and could not go where you wanted, but when you grow old you will be able to make your own decisions, go your own way, and control your own destiny." But Jesus has a different vision of maturity:

It is the ability and willingness to be led where you
would rather not go.[26]

Nouwen's words are not just for leaders. They are for all of
us. Many people "opt out" of following Jesus at precisely this
point. An unexpected, incomprehensible, often deeply painful
twist in the story occurs, and they turn back because they feel
the twist renders the whole enterprise a fraud, the whole story
meaningless.

I am here to tell you—it does not. You and I are not called
to have our stories under control. God neither needs nor desires
us to understand the meaning of them—at least not this side of
eternity, and maybe not there either. We are called to give and
keep giving ourselves to Jesus—and to the world he desperately
loves—regardless of the circumstances, "fixing our eyes," as the
writer of Hebrews says, "on Jesus, the pioneer and perfecter of
faith," who "for the joy set before him . . . endured the cross,
scorning its shame, and sat down at the right hand of the throne
of God."[27]

In his darkest hour, the Son of God yielded his will to the
deep and incomprehensible will of the Father. By the power
of the Holy Spirit, his obedient will can light up ours, making our own yielding possible, giving us hope that whatever
our circumstances, our lives have meaning, beyond what we
can see.

FOR REFLECTION

What are some areas of your life where you need, rather than
to fight, to enter into the gift and grace of self-abandonment?

PRAYER

Lord Jesus,
In your darkest hour,
you yielded your will
to the will of your Father,
ransoming humanity from death.
Help me also,
by the power of the Holy Spirit,
learn to yield my will,
for the Father's glory
and the world's good.
Amen.

THE HIDDEN FACE

Where can I flee from your presence?
PSALM 139:7

O dark of night, my guide!
night dearer than anything all your dawns discover!
O night drawing side to side
the loved and lover—
she that the lover loves, lost in the lover!

ST. JOHN OF THE CROSS, *"The Dark Night of the Soul"*

There are few things more wonderful than experiencing the presence of God. The Hebrew word commonly translated "presence" in the Old Testament happens to also mean "face." The word is *panim*.

Like the word *ruach*, the word *panim* has a rich, multivalent quality to it. The two primary meanings sit inside one another elegantly. Consider *panim* on the human level. When a person's face is turned toward you, so is their *being*, their *presence*. We grasp this intuitively. Have you ever been in conversation with someone, sharing a bit of your heart or a story about something that happened to you, only to watch their eyes and the orientation of their face wander to somewhere or someone else in the room? Where the eyes and the face go, so the presence goes. Relational contact has a great deal to do with the face.

As it is on the human level, so, as the ancient Hebrew writers grasped, it is with God: When the face of God is turned toward us, so also God is present to us. And what could be more wonderful or hopeful than having the gracious, life-giving face of the God Jesus would later call "Father" turned toward you? Thus, the psalmist made the face of God—his *panim*—the very height of human longing. Look for a moment at Psalm 27. The psalmist, David—no stranger to the experience of the presence of God—wrote,

> One thing I ask from the LORD,
>   this only do I seek:
> that I may dwell in the house of the LORD
>   all the days of my life,
> to gaze on the beauty of the LORD
>   and to seek him in his temple.
> For in the day of trouble
>   he will keep me safe in his dwelling;
> he will hide me in the shelter of his sacred tent
>   and set me high upon a rock.
>
> Then my head will be exalted
>   above the enemies who surround me;
> at his sacred tent I will sacrifice with shouts of joy;
>   I will sing and make music to the LORD.
>
> Hear my voice when I call, LORD;
>   be merciful to me and answer me.
> My heart says of you, "Seek his face!"
>   Your face, LORD, I will seek.

Do not hide your face from me,
  do not turn your servant away
    in anger;
  you have been my helper.
Do not reject me or forsake me,
  God my Savior.
Though my father and mother
    forsake me,
  the LORD will receive me.[1]

David believed that in the midst of all the hardship and trials of life, the favor of God's bright face was his best hope. If it turned toward him, life would go right. He knew that he could be rejected by everyone close to him—friends and family, father and mother—*but if the Lord* received him, his hope for a good future would be sure. Everything hung on the Face, the favor of the divine Presence.

This way of thinking about the presence of God was deeply embedded in the imagination of the Jewish people. To know the favor of God's face, his presence, was to know that life—whatever the circumstances—was ultimately going to work the way God intended. This was why the Lord told Moses to have the priests bless the people as follows:

The LORD bless you
  and keep you;
the LORD make his face shine on you
  and be gracious to you;
the LORD turn his face toward you
  and give you peace.

The Lord adds: "So they will put my name on the Israelites, *and I will bless them*."[2] Indeed. Where the divine face shines, there is peace, harmony, and blessing. To know and experience the *panim* of God is to know and experience *life*.

EXPERIENCING THE FACE

But what does it *mean* to "experience" the face, the presence, of God?

God, as we know, is not available to our naked sight. The apostle Paul wrote to his young protégé, Timothy, that God dwells in an "unapproachable light," and "no one has seen or can see" him.[3] God in his essence is hidden from our eyes. He is fundamentally different than we are. He is not a "thing" to be seen. We couldn't behold him directly if we tried.

Elsewhere Paul says that "in him we live and move and have our being."[4] God is, to put it one way, our deepest metaphysical *context*, our ultimate ontological *environment*. In chapter 1, I joked about addressing God as the "Ground of Being" instead of the name that Jesus gives us, *Father*. But don't take my joke to imply that God is *not* the Ground of Being. Indeed, he is always around us with his loving, omnibenevolent presence, willing and working our good—but not available to naked sight.

Understanding this, I think, helps us make sense of an interesting wrinkle in the Old Testament text. On the one hand, the *panim* of God was the height of human longing, and the priests invoked the favor of the *panim* in blessing over the Israelites. On the other hand, Yahweh says to Moses, "You cannot see my face, for no one may see me and live" and then hides Moses in the cleft of the rock while his glory passes by.[5] The Face may indeed bless and show favor, and it is for this Face that we long, but human eyes—God being what God is, and humans being what humans are—may not see it directly.

Grasping this leads us to one of the great and beautiful truths of the Christian vision of God—that God communicates himself to us with signs and hints and suggestions to awaken our hearts to his holy love. We *perceive* the face of God in those signs, hints, and suggestions by *faith*. Faith is one of the central things that mark off the believer from the unbeliever. In the grandeur and beauty of nature, faith sees the genius and joy of the Great Artist at work, his smile breaking across the morning skies or glimmering on the face of the waters. In the melody and harmony of music, faith hears the Singer's voice erupting in the song. In the rapture and ecstasy of falling in love, faith senses the presence of the Lord who in his triune being is Lover, Love, and Beloved.

Faith, though it cannot directly behold it, yet *perceives* the Presence. Faith "sees" the Face. And when it does, it is pure joy.

WHEN THE LIGHTS GO OUT

I can remember my initial awakenings to God like they were yesterday. Born and raised in a Christian home, I lived most of my life with a general *awareness* of God. I would even say that I had a *relationship* with God. I believed in and trusted in Jesus. But there comes a time in your life when God "breaks through" in a way that marks you forever, when God makes himself not just intellectually or theoretically real to you, but, well, *really real*—in a way that leaves no doubt.

That moment for me happened when I was a junior in high

school. In the midst of a season full of doubts and questions and a great deal of spiritual hunger, I found God. Or better, God found me. Or even better yet, *I found myself found by God.*

However you describe it (words are pretty limiting sometimes), what I can say for sure is that one morning before school, in my devotions, God crashed in, and I knew him to be the God the Bible speaks of when one of Jesus' best friends, John, writes that "God is love."[6]

It was an experience unlike any I had had up to that point, and it totally altered my way of seeing the world. Suddenly, every conversation, every interaction, every experience of corporate worship, every private devotion was for me a profound encounter with the living God. I saw him everywhere, in everything, effortlessly. For months.

And then just like that, as suddenly as it came, the lights went out. God vanished.

Or that's how I *felt.* Whatever the case, this divine vanishing act caught me completely off guard. Much of my upbringing had conditioned me to think that the "awakening" I had experienced months earlier was the beginning of a process that would take me—to use the words of Paul—from one experiential "degree of glory" to the next[7] until I died or the Lord Jesus himself returned. In my tradition, as in many, the *experiential* dimension of faith was prized. If your faith is working right—so we thought—you will experience *more* of God's presence, have *more* and *greater* revelation, and know *more* and *deeper dimensions* of intimacy with God. An unbroken, upward, experiential spiritual ascent. What else could "glory to glory" possibly mean?

We simply had no language for making sense of experiences of God's seeming absence. When you no longer see the Artist in his works, when you no longer hear the Singer in the song, when you no longer sense the Lover in the love, what then? What do you do when all consolation has evaporated, and your soul and senses are barren, arid, and dry? Where (if anywhere) is the God you have come to know as Father in that, and how do you make sense of it?

PEAKS AND TROUGHS

For me, the experience of what felt like the "absence" of God went on for an uncomfortably long time. Several years passed where for the life of me, despite all of my best efforts to regain the feelings that had marked my first awakening, I felt bereft. Worship services lacked savor; spiritual conversations seemed empty and hollow; even my devotional times seemed meaningless and futile. What was the point of any of it? I despaired.

Adding insult to injury was the gnawing sense that my situation was a result of personal failure—that I was doing something wrong. There *must* be—I thought—some fatal flaw in me rendering it impossible for me to experience God as I once had. My despair intensified. What was I to do?

I might have given up altogether had I not stumbled on C. S. Lewis's classic *The Screwtape Letters*—a brilliant fictional account of the attempt of two demons to undermine a recent convert to Christianity. At one point, Wormwood (the junior demon) reports glowingly to Screwtape (senior demon and mentor to Wormwood) of a period of spiritual aridity that his "patient" is experiencing. My own inner darkness notwithstanding, I had been enjoying the book immensely. This chapter, with its description of the spiritual condition of the young man, really piqued my interest.

To my surprise, Wormwood is not praised for his report. Instead, the much more experienced and world-wise Screwtape chastens the young tempter, saying, "The dryness and dullness through which your patient is now going are not, as you fondly suppose, your workmanship; *they are merely a natural phenomenon which will do us no good unless you make a good use of it.*"[8]

Wait, what? A "natural phenomenon"? Lewis had my curiosity there. To my mind, the whole *point* of the spiritual life was the unhindered elevation of our senses to the presence and glory of God. Anything else was surely hell's work or a sign of human failure. Lewis, however, seemed to think otherwise. In his mind, the ups and the downs of experience *had little to do with the actual health of a person's spiritual life.* For human beings, Screwtape observes, "to be in time means to change. Their nearest approach to constancy, therefore, is undulation—the repeated return to a level from which they repeatedly fall back, a series of troughs and peaks." Screwtape writes,

> If you had watched your patient carefully you would have seen this undulation in every department of his life—his interest in his work, his affection for his friends, his physical appetites, all go up and down. As long as he lives on earth periods of emotional and bodily richness and liveliness will alternate with periods of numbness and poverty.[9]

Why had I never noticed this before? Had I the eyes to see it, however, I would have spotted it everywhere. One notable place would have been my relationship with my wife. At the time, Mandi and I were in our first year or two of marriage. The initial "burst" of white-hot emotion—what some call "the honeymoon phase"—had begun to wane, and we were starting to settle in to the long work of learning to actually *love* one another with a love that was perhaps less explosive than it had once been, but more enduring; deeper and more solid than any teenage infatuation could ever be. Though I was growing comfortable and confident with that process in marriage, for some reason, I had not made the connection to my spiritual life.

Lewis was bringing to my attention a piece of Christian wisdom I had never seen before—namely, that in order for God to make us into the kind of persons he wants us to be, not only *does* he use periods of aridity and dryness (such as I was experiencing), but—more to the point—he *has* to use those experiences.

This is so, of course, not because of any constraint or limitation on God, but because, as Augustine said, our souls are restless until they rest and rest truly in God—not in *feelings* of God or even *ideas* of God, but in God himself, in union with the one who is at once the source of our very being, our ultimate metaphysical context, and our final goal. Screwtape continues his counsel to the young Wormwood:

It may surprise you to learn that in His efforts to get permanent possession of a soul, He relies on the troughs even more than on the peaks; some of His special favourites have gone through longer and deeper troughs than anyone else. The reason is this. To us a human is primarily food; our aim is the absorption of its will into ours, the increase of our own area of selfhood at its expense. But the obedience which the Enemy demands of men is quite a different thing. One must face the fact that all the talk about His love for men, and His service being perfect freedom, is not (as one would gladly believe) mere propaganda, but an appalling truth. He really *does* want to fill the universe with a lot of loathsome little replicas of Himself—creatures whose life, on its miniature scale, will be qualitatively like His own, not because He has absorbed them but because their wills freely conform to His.[10]

That being the case, Lewis contends (on the lips of old Uncle Screwtape) that the one thing God *cannot* do is override our wills. His whole program depends on his refusal to achieve his goals by destroying us. "He cannot ravish," writes Screwtape. "He can only woo." And then the lines that stopped me cold:

He is prepared to do a little overriding at the beginning. He will set them off with communications of His presence which, though faint, seem great to them, with emotional sweetness, and easy conquest over temptation. But He never allows this state of affairs to last long. Sooner or later He withdraws, if not in fact, at least from their conscious experience, all those supports and incentives. He leaves the creature to stand up on its own legs—to carry out from the will alone duties which have lost all relish. It is during such trough periods, much more than during the peak periods, that it is growing into the sort of creature He wants it to be. . . . Our cause is never more in danger than when a human, no longer desiring, but still intending, to do our Enemy's will, looks round upon a universe from which every trace of Him seems to have vanished, and asks why he has been forsaken, and still obeys.[11]

THE DARK NIGHT OF THE SOUL

Suddenly my spiritual life had hope again. No, I was not "experiencing" the bright, smiling face of God as I once had. Yet something in me told me that what was happening in me was good. Very good, even. As with my marriage, I was being liberated from the fluctuations of experience in order to enter the depths of real love—a love that endured in obedient faithfulness even when it couldn't "feel" God. A purification was taking place. My faith was being forged at a deeper level. Deeper than feelings and sense perception, beyond pious religious sentiment—I was learning to see, to love, to know and be known, in the pitch dark.

It turns out that all the great spiritual masters have understood that this is a crucial element of the journey of faith. No real maturity is attained without it. Richard Foster writes that "times of seeming desertion and absence and abandonment appear to be universal among those who have walked this path of faith before us," going on to recommend that "we might just as well get used to the idea that, sooner or later, we, too, will know what it means to feel forsaken by God."[12]

Cast even a brief glance at church history, and you'll see Foster's comments validated everywhere. The anonymous

English author of the fourteenth-century work *The Cloud of Unknowing* claimed that in order to really know the Lord, one must pass through a certain darkening of the intellect, senses, and emotions, learning, from a place of pure desire, to "beat on that thick cloud of unknowing with the sharp arrow of longing and never stop loving, no matter what comes your way."[13]

In a similar vein, the seventeenth-century bishop of Geneva St. Francis de Sales asserted that much of our spiritual dryness, especially in prayer, is the Lord's purifying work in us. "Prayer," he wrote, "illumines our understanding with a divine light, and lays open our will to the holy flames of celestial love. Nothing so much purifies our mind from its errors, or our will from its depraved affections."[14] A lovely sentiment, no doubt, and—one should note—easily misunderstood, for Francis goes on to explain that one of the things we must be purified of is what he terms "excessive ardor" that mistakes "a *perception* of God" for God, that mistakes "a *feeling* of faith" for faith.[15] For Francis, to *sense* God or to *perceive* God is not the same as *having* God; to *feel* faith is not the same as *having* faith.

How many of us, I wonder, genuinely understand this? For many, the health of our spirituality is measured by the intensity of our religious emotions. We have a particularly illuminating or inspiring devotional time and feel as though our faith is therefore sound. We come out of a worship service that awakened us to a profound sense of the transcendent or led to feelings of deep spiritual consolation and believe therefore that all is right with us. But is it? The spiritual masters tend to be skeptical of the value of mere religious experience. What are our motives? What does all the emotion *lead* to, if anything at all? Where is the fruit, and what is it? They seem to think that in the spiritual life there are bigger fish to fry than chasing gooey emotional experiences.

We must, the masters counsel us, love God for God's sake—not for what he gives to us. Many, of course, love God for the promise that loving God will make their lives prosperous and healthy. While we may be tempted to jeer the rank materialism of this approach to God, it is important to realize that we ourselves may be, in fact, rank materialists on a more subtle and therefore more insidious level. We may not love God for the promise of having a larger house and a healthier body; instead, we love God for the promise of *happy feelings* and *spiritual illumination*—which, we should note, *are also created and finite and therefore, so to speak, "material" things.*

If such is the case, then it turns out that we don't really love God for God's sake, after all. We love him for what he gives—in this case, feelings. *But here's the paradox:* When we learn to love God not for anything he gives but for who he is—the triune God, in whom we live and move and have our being—it leads us into the most profound "knowing" of God available to human beings (and often, it should be noted, to more profound and deeper feelings). We start moving toward deep union with God—not in spite of but *because of* and *through* the darkness. We begin to see, with Jacob, that not only is God in "this place" (wherever we might be) but that he is in *every* place, even when we are not sensibly aware of it.

And right there yet another paradox unfolds. Having grasped the truth that God is powerfully and graciously present in every place even when we are not *sensibly* aware of it, *we become all the more aware of it*—by the apprehension of pure faith. Could anything be more blessed than this, than our spirits' happy inner beholding of the enfolding divine Presence?

This is what makes the periodic veiling of God to our senses a *gift*, a *grace*. Perhaps the finest expression of this understanding comes from the sixteenth-century Spanish priest St. John of the Cross. John believed that God frequently used what he called "the dark night of the soul" to lead people to union with him. During the experience of the "dark night," John contends, God "weans" the soul "from . . . sweetnesses and pleasures," giving it instead "pure aridities and inward darkness," which, if endured patiently, allow the soul to "win the virtues"[16]—faith, hope, and love.

Such faith, hope, and love, he contends, are not dependent on feelings or circumstances, but instead are anchored in the reality of God himself—the "I am" of the biblical record whose very being simply *is* and *is always* regardless of our feelings or circumstances. For John, it is precisely this darkness that leads us into that deepest union with God, whereby our lives are transformed. Paradoxically, joy and freedom reach their fullness in our spirits on the far side of this divine weaning process. John writes of this "dark night of the soul" in metaphors that would be almost irreverent if the imagery did not emerge from Scripture (particularly the Song of Songs):

> *There in the lucky dark,*
> *none to observe me, darkness far and wide;*
> *no sign for me to mark,*
> *no other light, no guide*
> *except for my heart—the fire, the fire inside!*

That led me on
true as the very noon is—truer too!—
to where there waited one
I knew—how well I knew!—
in a place where no one was in view.

O dark of night, my guide!
night dearer than anything all your dawns discover!
O night drawing side to side
the loved and lover—
she that the lover loves, lost in the lover! . . .

In air from the castle wall
as my hand in his hair moved lovingly at play,
he let cool fingers fall
—and the fire there where they lay!—
all senses in oblivion drift away.[17]

For John, the stripping of the senses by means of this spiritual darkness is the method God uses to bring us to deep union with him, enabling us to perceive God not only in sweetness and pleasure but also—more importantly—in times of abandonment and desolation. We come to see in *un*-seeing, to know in *un*-knowing. We learn to embrace periodic seasons of aridity and dryness as gifts of grace—as God drawing close to us and drawing us close to him. Which is why, in fact, John likens our times of spiritual darkness to the physical darkness that lovers seek in the pursuit of intimacy. Thus he calls this darkness "the *lucky* dark" and the "night *dearer*" than "all your dawns" because it "draw[s] side to side the loved and lover."

In the darkness, according to John, deep faith, deep intimacy, deep union is forged. Our whole being becomes increasingly "one" with God. And it is a faith that—*just because* it is not dependent on happy feelings or sensible experiences of God's presence or on things going the way they ought—is, by that very fact, unshakable. It is, strange as it may sound, a gift, a grace. Because it paradoxically sees the face of God in the pitch-darkness, because it paradoxically perceives the presence of God in what the ancients called the *Deus absconditus* (the absence of God), because it paradoxically "knows" God even in the *un*-knowing, it is a faith that is utterly secure.

This is the kind of faith that God desires for us. Not an infantile emotivism, but a rock-steady confidence that *God is* and that *God is for me*—however I feel and whatever the circumstance. The Father of our Lord Jesus Christ is the exalted God of heaven and earth who, *because* he is the Ground of Being, does not flit in and out of our lives like the gods of the pagans, but is always closer to us than our very breath, nearer to us in his burning kindness than our very skin. The faithful know this and build their lives accordingly.

GOD-FORSAKEN GOD

Coming to grips with this truth helped my faith immensely back in those days. It helps me still. I found and am finding that I can rest in the dulling of my senses and the periodic drying out of my soul without panicking. The prophet Isaiah's words have since taken on a new significance for me:

Who among you fears the LORD
 and obeys the word of his servant?
Let the one who walks in the dark,
 who has no light,
trust in the name of the LORD
 and rely on their God.[18]

Trusting God, I have come to see, is not the same as "sensing" or "perceiving" the presence of God. Now, don't misunderstand me here. I *love* times when I can sense and perceive the presence of God. When my heart burns in prayer and tears fall easily in worship, when the Scriptures sing with the music of eternity and spiritual conversation flows naturally, when sight and taste and sound all remind me of the thousand different ways the face of God has turned toward me, when pure spiritual ecstasy washes over me—those are wonderful times, and I thank God for them.

But I have learned that I must also love and cherish the times of darkness, for they, paradoxically, make it possible for me to sense and perceive the *panim* at a deeper and more important level. The heroes of biblical faith have all, in their way, walked this path before us. They were no strangers to times of divine obscurity. God, the Scripture says, revealed himself and his plans long ago to Abraham in a "thick and dreadful darkness."[19] The psalmist said that "clouds and thick darkness surround him [the LORD]."[20] The righteous Job complained in the midst of a terrifyingly dark period, "When he passes me, I cannot see him; when he goes by, I cannot perceive him"[21]—and yet believed that God was *there*, incomprehensibly but truly. At one point, David, who certainly knew the sweetness of the

Lord's presence, lamented that the Lord had made the darkness his "closest friend."[22]

Learning to know and love the Lord in the darkness—you and I are on solid biblical ground there, friend. The apostle Paul said that we know and walk with the Lord not "by sight" but "by faith."[23] Put in the language of this chapter—we do not walk by a "sense" of God's presence, or by "feelings" of his favor or "feelings" even of doctrinal or metaphysical certitude. It is folly to hang your relationship with God on such things. We walk by faith. Period.

As a pastor I have often sat with people who lamented to me that they were "losing" their faith. I have had dozens and perhaps hundreds of tearful meetings with folks who despaired that their grip on their faith was slowly slipping away. As I've listened to these poor souls pour out their hearts, more often than not what I find is that the "dark night" that leads us directly to God is descending, but these precious people do not know what to do with it because they've placed their faith not in God himself but in their *feelings* about God—and no one has counseled them otherwise. Could it be that in times when we think that we are "losing" our faith, the very "faith" that we are losing is a faith that needs to be burned away so that a genuine confidence in the living God—the God who *is* and is beyond our feelings about him—might emerge?

We ought to at least consider the possibility, for men and women across history, geography, and culture have walked through darkness just like (and often so much worse than) ours, and come out better for it. Breathe easy in such times, friend; you're in good company.

One last example before I conclude this chapter. It is one I turn to often when I am feeling desolate and abandoned. Have you ever considered the Lord Jesus himself? Son of the Father though he was, on whom the divine Face from eternity to eternity smiles, from the cross all those centuries ago, yet cried out, *"My God, my God, why have you forsaken me?"*[24]

Think about it: *God has tasted God-forsakenness.* God has known God-abandonment. God has known divine absence. God has seen the face of God turn away. God has walked with humanity in the valley of the shadow of death, has stood with us in the cold mists of un-knowing.

And that means something for you and me—for all who walk through times of desolation and darkness. One of my favorite psalms has always been Psalm 139. Listen to what David says:

> Where can I go from your Spirit?
> Where can I flee from your presence?
> If I go up to the heavens, you are there;
> if I make my bed in the depths, you are there.
> If I rise on the wings of the dawn,
> if I settle on the far side of the sea,
> even there your hand will guide me,
> your right hand will hold me fast.
> If I say, "Surely the darkness will hide me
> and the light become night around me,"
> even the darkness will not be dark to you;
> the night will shine like the day,
> for darkness is as light to you.[25]

David wrote better than he knew. Darkness—whether that darkness be spiritual, psychological, or circumstantial—cannot be a terror to us because God in Christ has taken the darkness into himself and filled it with his light. I have learned and am learning that because that is so—because in Christ, God has taken the *entire* human experience into himself—when life is rosy and my heart is full of hope and positivity, when God's face seems obvious and evident everywhere, I can give thanks. That is surely a gift from the Father above, "who does not change like shifting shadows."[26]

And by the same token, I have learned and am learning that in times of what feels like abandonment and forsakenness, when my soul is arid and dry and the face of God seems hidden, deeper faith is being formed in me, and the fruit is sure to follow: *love, joy, peace, forbearance, kindness, goodness, faithfulness, gentleness, and self-control.*[27] The Spirit is making me a flame.

Even more—I know that in those times of seeming abandonment and absence, I have a companion: the Son of God himself, who knows what it is to be human, waiting in the dark for God.

FOR REFLECTION

Is anything in this chapter changing the way you think about times of spiritual darkness? If so, how?

PRAYER

Almighty God, heavenly Father,
Who everywhere and always surrounds us,
Open my eyes to your hidden presence.
Anchor me in your goodness,
not only in times of light
but also in the darkness.
Use it to make me one with you.
Amen.

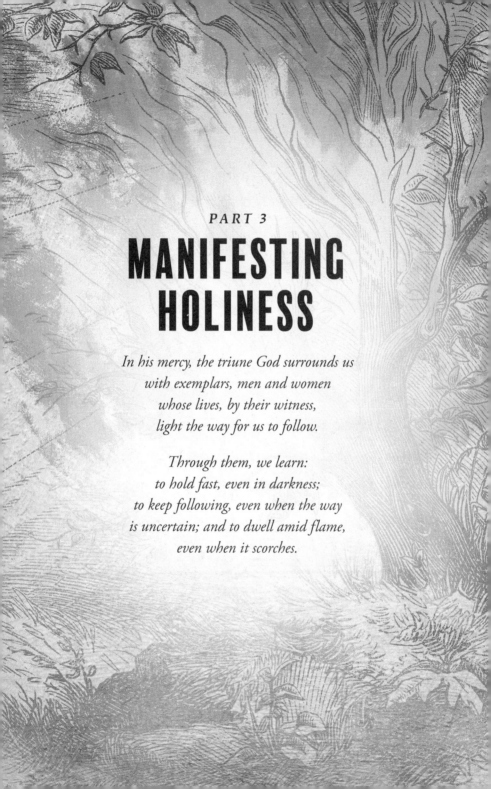

PART 3

MANIFESTING HOLINESS

*In his mercy, the triune God surrounds us
with exemplars, men and women
whose lives, by their witness,
light the way for us to follow.*

*Through them, we learn:
to hold fast, even in darkness;
to keep following, even when the way
is uncertain; and to dwell amid flame,
even when it scorches.*

TO OFFER GOD THE EMPTINESS

Mother Teresa

[Teresa] radiated remarkable joy and love. She was truly a witness to hope, an apostle of love and joy, because she had built the edifice of her life on pure faith. She glowed with a kind of "luminosity."

BRIAN KOLODIEJCHUK, *Mother Teresa: Come Be My Light*

If I ever become a saint—I will surely be one of "darkness."
I will continually be absent from heaven—to light
the light of those in darkness on earth.

MOTHER TERESA to her spiritual director,
Father Joseph Neuner (March 6, 1962)

As we have seen, when the Lord first comes to us, he comes with a profound awakening to his delightful presence. We come alive to the love of the Father, which begins a process of overwhelming and healing our brokenness, making us radiant with his character, which is love.

Part of this process includes experiences of desolation and inward abandonment. We walk through times when the divine Face is veiled to our senses. Though disorienting and terrifying at first, we begin to see where and how God is at work in the darkness, forging deeper faith in us, making us more fully the kinds of persons he desires us to be. And, we saw, we can take deep solace in the fact that we have a companion in darkness—the Son of God himself, who shared our abandonment, crying out from the cross, "My God, my God, why have you forsaken me?" No better companion could we ask for.

All of this sounds very good on paper, but is it true? you might be wondering. *Show me someone who lived it, who patiently endured it, whose life was radiant because of it. Show me someone whose experience bears witness to what you are saying.*

Happily. Let me introduce you to one of the great modern saints: Mother Teresa of Calcutta, who once said to her spiritual director that if she ever became a saint, she would surely be one of darkness, yet whose life lit up the world with the radiant love of God. I can think of no better person to illustrate how God uses inner darkness to transform us and the world around us.

TERESA'S EARLY LIFE AND CALL

On August 26, 1910, Agnes Gonxha Bojaxhiu was born in Skopje (now the capital of North Macedonia) to Albanian parents, Nikola and Dranafile, the youngest of three children. By all accounts the Bojaxhiu family enjoyed a happy life together. Agnes's older brother, Lazar, recalled it as "peaceful and pleasant."[1] Nikola, their father, was a prosperous businessman and civic leader. Drana, their mother, was an industrious and attentive homemaker. A devout Catholic family, the Bojaxhius were hardworking, self-disciplined, and unhesitatingly generous. When a poor elderly woman began to frequent their house for meals, Nikola instructed them, "Welcome her warmly, with love. . . . Never eat a single mouthful unless you are sharing it with others."[2]

In 1919, crisis hit. The sudden death of Nikola fell like a hammerblow on Drana and her three children. Their wealth evaporated, and before long, they were left nearly destitute. Drana's strong spirit shone, however. Doing all she could both to provide for her children and to maintain the family's ethos, Drana set a powerful example for the future saint of Calcutta. One biographer explains,

> It was very largely under the influence of her
> devout mother, and her insistence on the value
> of the nonmaterial riches of kindness, generosity
> and compassion for the poor and weak, that the
> foundations for Agnes's future apostolate were laid.[3]

The family continued to welcome the poor and the destitute, and before long, a sense of calling took shape in Agnes. At twelve she had "an intensely personal experience on which she would not elaborate."[4] Though she would often explain that it was not a vision, we know based on what would follow that this "intensely personal experience" was spiritual in nature and that it revealed to her God's heart for the world and his will for her life: to love God by serving the poor.

For the next six years, Agnes wrestled with what the total devotion of her life to God would look like, eventually becoming enthralled with the stories told by her local parish priest, Father Jambrekovic, of the work of a group of Yugoslavian priests in the archdiocese of Calcutta among the poorest of the poor. By eighteen she was convinced that India was where she belonged. She applied to join the Loreto Sisters, an Irish branch of the Institute of the Blessed Virgin Mary, who were also hard at work in Calcutta. She was accepted, and so her journey of following Christ to bring light and hope into the most desolate places of human life began.

THE THIRST OF JESUS

The first leg of Agnes's journey was to Loreto Abbey in Rathfarnham, Ireland, to learn English. After six short weeks in Ireland, she and one other postulant made their way to India. Along the way, Agnes chose the name under which she would later become famous—Teresa, after Thérèse of Lisieux, the nineteenth-century French saint who was known for her emphasis on loving Jesus by honoring him in "small things." Though Mother Teresa's life ultimately would not, by any stretch of the imagination, be considered a "small thing," it was certainly predicated on such fidelity.

When she arrived in India in 1929, Teresa's assignment was to teach—first in and around Darjeeling in the lower Himalayas and then later in Calcutta. Teaching exposed her in a unique way to the lives of the poor, and it was then that Teresa's character and calling truly began to emerge. Not only was she a hard and competent worker, an excellent teacher, and a joyful and happy colleague; she also demonstrated a unique compassion for those whose lives were ravaged by poverty. The work of the Loreto nuns was to combat poverty through education, so Teresa's work put her in intimate and daily proximity to the poorest of the poor.

By all accounts, they loved her. And she loved them. And hurt for them. When, in 1937, Teresa took her vows of poverty, chastity, and obedience, becoming thereby "Mother" Teresa, one of the slum children who had fallen in love with her worried aloud that he was afraid her new commitments would take her away from them:

> He began to cry, and through his tears he said, "Oh, don't become Mother!" I held him to me and asked him, "What is the matter? Do not worry. I will be back. I will always be your Ma."[5]

"I held him to me" would in time become the signature of Mother Teresa's unique affection for the poor. Teresa's affection was not intellectual or detached; rather, she expressed it in gentle touch, compassionate eyes, and a tender smile that communicated to its recipients that they were valuable, that they were human, that they were *wanted*. She took joy in them, and they in her. A friend of hers remarked, "What drew countless numbers of people to love and admire Mother Teresa, over many years, was the manifest joy which shone in her every gesture"—especially toward those who were poor or destitute in any way.[6]

Teresa's affection for the poor grew as the years went by. The Bengal famine of 1943 and the eruption of Muslim-Hindu violence in Calcutta in 1946 brought new suffering to the city, and with it, new burdens for Teresa. Now the principal of St. Mary's school and the de facto superior of the Daughters of St. Anne (the Loreto nuns' affiliate Bengali congregation), she began to feel that more was being asked of her. When violence between Muslims and Hindus broke out in Calcutta on "The Day of Great Killing" in August of 1946, leaving thousands dead and many critically injured, Teresa, with hundreds of hungry pupils and workers under her care, chose to risk her life by heading out into the violent, bloodstained streets to find food for them.

A group of soldiers met her there, admonishing her to return indoors. When she explained her situation, the soldiers (surely astounded at the courage of this small woman) drove her back to the school and unloaded bags of rice for her and her pupils to eat. That was Teresa—a small woman whose large love moved the world.

It was during this time that the call to establish the Missionaries of Charity came. On a train ride to Darjeeling for her annual retreat in September of 1946, Teresa sensed what she would later come to describe as "the call within the call." She explained,

> [It] was a call within my vocation. It was a second
> calling. It was a vocation to give up even Loreto where I
> was very happy and to go out in the streets to serve the
> poorest of the poor. It was in that train, I heard the call
> to give up all and follow Him into the slums—to serve
> Him in the poorest of the poor. . . . I knew it was His
> will and that I had to follow Him. There was no doubt
> that it was going to be His work.[7]

She would return from her retreat and immediately begin a process of discernment with her superiors regarding the validity and nature of this work. From the outset, Teresa was clear— the missionary congregation to be founded would be defined by one thing: satiating the "thirst" of Jesus. "*The General End* of the Missionaries of Charity," read one of the first drafts of the rules for the new congregation, "is to satiate the thirst of Jesus Christ on the Cross for Love and Souls."[8] The God revealed in Jesus, Teresa grasped with great clarity, was a God who "thirsted" both *to* love and to *be* loved. The poor were unique objects of his "thirst." Not

only did God ache *to love the poor*, whose lives had been strip
of all dignity, with his dignifying grace, but God, Teresa und
stood, ached *to be loved in the poor* by those he had called to sei
them. The entire exchange was grounded in the mystery of ti
Incarnation—how God, in Christ, out of love, had taken human
ity's broken flesh into himself to bless and heal it.

The Missionaries of Charity would soon embody that mystery of incarnate love in a way the world had rarely (if ever)
seen. Compelled by the infinite love of God, the M. C. sisters
would carry the light of Christ into the darkest holes of humanity, giving of themselves in a way that made the character
of God evident in all they did. "Charity," Teresa taught, "is
love, it's a giving; like God loved the world, He gave His Son
. . . so if we really love . . . we must give until it hurts."[9] Teresa
often explained that M. C. sisters were not social workers but
"contemplatives in the world" who both brought and sought
the mystery of God's dignifying love to and among those whose
lives had been bereft of it—whether or not they ever came to
personally know and love the Jesus who reveals God. This conviction was uniquely expressed by Teresa when, commenting on
the M. C. work taking place at Nirmal Hriday, a home for the
dying, she said, "A beautiful death is for people who lived like
animals to die like angels—loved and wanted."[10]

THE PARALLEL STORY—TERESA'S DARKNESS

For the next fifty years, Teresa and the Missionaries of Charity
would work tirelessly to spread the love of God to the most
desolate people and places on planet Earth. "By the time of
her death in 1997, the Missionaries of Charity numbered more

than 4,000—in addition to thousands more lay volunteers—with 610 foundations in 123 countries around the world."[11]

On that pivotal train ride to Darjeeling in 1946, the Lord had told her, *"Come, come, carry Me into the holes of the poor. Come, be My light."*[12] Fifty years later, Teresa's efforts had done just that—the world was ablaze with the fires of dignifying, divine love that she had lit; fires that illuminated not only Earth's dark places but also places of prestige and halls of power. Kings, queens, diplomats, presidents—the influential of every stripe, the most powerful of the powerful—routinely sought out Teresa for the wisdom, guidance, and light that her life provided.

What few knew was the excruciating darkness Teresa carried within.

Almost immediately following her death, Pope John Paul II, an ardent admirer of Teresa and vocal supporter of her work, initiated the process of beatifying and canonizing her. Father Brian Kolodiejchuk, an M. C. brother, was appointed postulator.[13] In examining hundreds of pieces of private correspondence between Teresa and her spiritual directors over the course of her long life, a fuller picture began to emerge. Not only was Teresa utterly surrendered to God and his will for her life—that much everyone knew—but, more amazingly, she was so in spite of the fact that for more than fifty years, she had lived with what might be described as St. John of the Cross's "dark night of the soul." Whatever it was, it was certainly a piercing spiritual desolation. The woman who had lit the world with the love of God, doing all she could to ensure that the God-forsaken of the world would know they were loved and wanted, had herself endured perhaps the longest period of inward abandonment we have

on record, searching in the darkness for even a scrap of divine consolation—anything to remind her of the Lord's sweet love and desire for her—and finding little to none.

The inner darkness began almost immediately following the founding of the M. C. Called by the Lord to bring the light of his love to the unloved and unwanted, Teresa experienced her departure from the Loreto sisters as a sore trial. Loreto had been a place of security for her—a second family where she was surrounded by warm relationships and meaningful work. She was now striking out into the unknown. It pained her terribly. In a journal entry shortly after the founding of the M. C., she wrote,

> Today I learned a good lesson—the poverty of the poor must be often so hard for them. When I went rounding looking for a home—I walked and walked till my legs and my arms ached—I thought how they must also ache in body and soul looking for home—food—help—Then the temptation grew strong—the palace buildings of Loreto came rushing into my mind—all the beautiful things and comforts—the people they mix with—in a word everything.—"You have only to say a word and all that will be yours again"—the tempter kept on saying. Of [my] free choice My God and out of love for you— I desire to remain and do what ever be Your Holy Will in my regard.—I did not let a single tear come.—Even if I suffer more than now,—I still want to do Your Holy Will. This is the dark night of the birth of the Society— My God give me courage now—this moment—to persevere in following Your call.[14]

Teresa desired to follow God by immersing herself in the conditions of the poor, identifying completely with those whose lives had been reduced to nothing—even if it meant her own personal suffering and anguish.

And anguish it certainly was. She was just beginning to taste it. Before long Teresa would come to experience the anguish not only as the result of the change in her surroundings but as a deep inner desolation that persisted in spite of the rapid success of the work. When outwardly there was every sign of God's blessing and favor, inwardly she felt bereft. "Your Grace," she wrote to the Archbishop of Calcutta in 1953, "please pray specially for me that I may not spoil His work and that Our Lord may show Himself—for there is such terrible darkness within me, as if everything was dead. It has been like this more or less from the time I started 'the work.' Ask Our Lord to give me courage. Please give us Your blessing."[15]

Private pleas like this would continue. A year after she had first made her desolation known to the archbishop, she wrote him again, saying, "My own soul remains in deep darkness & desolation. No I don't complain—let Him do with me whatever He wants."[16] Kolodiejchuk explains, "Surrendering anew, she sacrificed willingly the consolation of felt union with Jesus for the challenge of living by pure faith. This experience made her even more understanding and compassionate toward others, enabling her to offer encouragement and practical advice."[17]

Clearly, something profound was at work in Teresa. Even if and while she was inwardly destitute, still it was evident to those around her that her union with Christ was growing, producing the life-giving fruit of compassion, tenderness, and courage so desperately needed in the God-forsaken slums of Calcutta. The darkness was doing its work in this saintly woman. Ten years after the Lord first called her to establish the M. C., she wrote that "within me everything is icy cold. . . . It is only that blind faith that carries me through for in reality to me all is darkness." But, she added, "As long as Our Lord has all the pleasure—I really do not count."[18] Teresa, who had sacrificed so much already, was learning to rise even higher above self-regard, abandoning herself completely to the Lord and to the people he had called her to serve.

As the years went by, the suffering continued unabated. In her private correspondence she talked often about the torture and pain of wanting God and yet feeling like God no longer wanted her. Still, she pressed on, determined to quench the thirst of Jesus by extending his love into the world and by loving him passionately in the poverty-ravaged bodies of the poor. She ached to love the God revealed in Jesus like he had never been loved before.

THE HIDDEN SOURCE

Love him she did. And in time, though the darkness did not subside, her understanding of it did. Teresa began to see that the darkness was not simply a purification but the price of fulfilling the work the Lord had called her to. Kolodiejchuk calls it a "martyrdom of desire" that only grew in intensity. Once after witnessing the pain and grief of a young girl crying out for her mother, Teresa wrote to her spiritual director, "I wish I could suffer more spiritually—if this would give her relief."[19] She was prepared to experience even *more* desolation if it would serve those Christ had given his life for. She loved them, and she loved him, *that much*. Christ, at Golgotha, had given all for her and for them. How could she give any less?

And it was that identification with the very suffering of Christ on the cross that began to grow in Teresa through her darkness. As the years went by, new dimensions of her desolation began to open to her. She noted to one spiritual director, "I have come to love the darkness—For I believe now that it is a part, a very, very small part of Jesus' darkness & pain on earth."[20] Teresa saw that on the cross, Christ Jesus had gathered up the physical and spiritual desolation of every human being into his body, identifying himself perfectly with them. Her darkness was a taste of Christ's agony for an agonized humanity and therefore a mysterious gift that put her in deepest contact with the God revealed in Jesus. It was this understanding that enabled her to write to a friend, "With me the *sunshine of darkness is bright*."[21]

The growth of Teresa's understanding of her darkness drove her deeper into her calling, with ever greater energy and strength. The paradoxical quality of this is captured well by her biographer Kathryn Spink, who notes how often the words "and yet" occur in the letters of Teresa:

On the one hand, her desire for God.

And yet . . . such desolation.

On the one hand, the desolation.

And yet . . . Jesus so evidently present, visible in the faces of the poor whom she wholeheartedly embraced.

On the one hand, Jesus' presence in the faces of the poor.

And yet . . . her soul still ached to be embraced by God as she once embraced the slum child when she took her religious vows so many years earlier.[22]

She was living in the paradox of presence-in-absence and absence-in-presence that the saints and mystics of old had spoken of. Father Paul Murray explains that "the terrible darkness she endured for so long—that long night which seemed so empty of love and empty of meaning—was, at its deepest core, nothing less, in fact, than the mysterious and brilliant light—the paradoxical *sunshine*—of God's presence."[23]

As the years went by, Teresa's sanctity increased. One spiritual director of Teresa's in the 1970s commented, "Whenever I met Mother, all self-consciousness left me. I felt right away at ease: she radiated peace and joy. . . . I could not help but think: Here is a person God dreamed of in Paradise, truly a touch of God. Yet I have to say at the same time that she was one of the most down-to-earth persons I have ever met."[24]

Teresa was a woman radiant with the gritty, down-to-earth, others-preferring, humble glory of the incarnate and crucified Son of God. The inner darkness had largely been responsible for shaping this in her. And she recognized it. At eighty-five years old, nearing the end of her life, Teresa commented to a friend, "What a wonderful gift from God to be able to offer Him the emptiness I feel. I am so happy to give Him this gift."[25]

By the time her life was over, she had—extraordinarily as it may seem—*befriended* the darkness. It was, as it turns out, her hidden source of light.

It is tempting to use the story of Mother Teresa as a sort of template for the spiritual life. I think, frankly, that to do so would be a mistake. Not everyone will walk through darkness like she did. In fact, as I noted earlier, Teresa's desolation lasted longer and went deeper than perhaps anyone's we have on record. Moreover, Teresa herself was never forthcoming publicly about her darkness, generally revealing it only to those who were charged with her spiritual and practical care—superiors and spiritual directors who, so she judged, *needed to know*. She was adamant that her life was not the point—Jesus was. Accordingly, she was afraid that knowledge of her experience would distract from Jesus and from the beautiful, ongoing work of the Missionaries of Charity among the poor. Such humility.

For those reasons, we must handle her story with care. The reason I chose it to complete our look at this dimension of the spiritual journey is because—despite her protestations, and despite its uniqueness both in duration and in depth—Teresa's story provides some powerful signposts for us when we walk through our own times of desolation.

First, Teresa's experience is a reminder that God routinely uses darkness to deepen and strengthen us in faith. Let us never forget that. Hard as it may seem, it is indispensable. Through the darkness we shed our dependence on feelings and learn to lean onto and into the Lord in pure faith and complete surrender to his will. As we do, the light in us grows.

Second, Teresa's experience is a reminder that the lack of a sense of inward consolation is not a sign that our faith is

malfunctioning. It is one of the commonest and most dangerous errors in the church to believe that the life of holiness is
a life of unbroken spiritual ecstasy, and that anything less is
surely evidence that we are out of God's favor and love, that
our union with him is defunct. St. Teresa of Calcutta, who
lives now in the immediate presence of the God she loved and
served her whole life, is a living repudiation of that notion.
The stripping of the senses may be a sign that your faith is
working better than you realize. Just hold on, like Teresa,
offering God the emptiness you feel, for God, dear one, is
holding on to you.

And finally, Teresa's experience is a reminder that we can
befriend the darkness because we *have* a Friend who drank the
cup of humanity's darkness—Christ the Lord, companion in
our sorrows, who cried out from the cross, "My God, my
God, why have you forsaken me?" Saints and spiritual masters
down through the ages have insisted that inner darkness puts
us in touch in a unique way with the darkness Jesus tasted as
one of us, for us, to lead humanity triumphantly home to the
Father's love, so that there is nowhere we can go to flee from
his presence.

For with him, even the darkness is full of holy light.

As the psalmist said, "Where can I go from your Spirit?
Where can I flee from your presence?"[26]

May you ever remember that.

FOR REFLECTION

Looking back, how has God used times of darkness and dryness
to deepen and strengthen your faith?

PRAYER

Gracious God,
Thank you for the example
of Mother Teresa's life.
Work in me
the same fruits
you worked in her—
compassion, tenderness,
kindness, humility—
and when I walk through
the valley of the shadow
like she did,
teach me to cling to you.
Amen.

8

TO ENTER THE UNKNOWN
Dietrich Bonhoeffer

Discipleship means adherence to the person of Jesus, and therefore submission to the law of Christ which is the law of the cross.

DIETRICH BONHOEFFER, *The Cost of Discipleship*

At the place of execution, he again said a short prayer and then climbed the steps to the gallows, brave and composed. . . . In the almost fifty years that I worked as a doctor, I have hardly ever seen a man die so entirely submissive to the will of God.

A WITNESS TO THE MARTYRDOM
OF DIETRICH BONHOEFFER

To yield to the Lord Jesus Christ is to have our lives upended. The earliest Christians believed that salvation was far more than simply "accepting Jesus into my heart." For them, it was about throwing their lives into the rollicking adventure of cosmic renewal God had inaugurated in the life, death, and resurrection of Jesus, the revolutionary prophet from Nazareth in Galilee. To say yes to Jesus, to answer his call, "Follow me," was about *that*—and it required a radical rethinking of a person's whole existence. It still does.

The temptation is to believe that at some point we will graduate from the costly call to deny ourselves, take up our cross, and follow him. That once we've taken enough risks and proven that we can successfully handle them, we'll be able to sit back, relax, and enjoy the good life. What we find—much to our astonishment—is that Christ the Lord keeps calling us deeper, into costlier acts of obedience, grittier acts of faithfulness, where the path often becomes even more unknown, obscure, and incomprehensible. As we saw, it is often circumstances beyond our control that push us into these costly acts of obedience. How do we respond when we find ourselves in a story we did not expect, would not have chosen, and do not fully understand? What happens when, in the ebb and flow of our lives, the way becomes obscure; when we no longer see the road stretching out for miles but perhaps inches—maybe—in front of us? What then?

In my life, I have not encountered a single believer of substance who has not faced this "crisis" of faith—often many times over. I am now firmly convinced that it is simply part of the job description of following the Lord Jesus Christ.

Church history provides plentiful examples of this. Let me introduce you to one of my favorite and (arguably) one of the most compelling models of the kind of faith that follows Jesus into the crisis of unknowing, the faith that yields ever and anew to the Lord in the midst of the unexpected and incomprehensible: the German pastor, theologian, and martyr Dietrich Bonhoeffer.

EARLY LIFE

Most of us know Bonhoeffer as the courageous Nazi-resister who penned the famous and (for him) prophetic words "When Christ calls a man, he bids him come and die."[1] Fewer of us are aware of the unfolding revelation of the personal call of Christ that took him there.

Dietrich Bonhoeffer was born in 1906 to Karl and Paula Bonhoeffer in Breslau, Germany. He had a twin sister, Sabine, and they were the sixth and seventh of eight children. Dietrich's childhood was destined to be charmed.

The Bonhoeffers represented the upper crust of German society. Karl was a prominent and well-respected psychiatrist and neurologist whose father, Friedrich, had been a similarly respected judicial official in the German state of Württemberg in the mid-to-late nineteenth century and whose mother, Julie, hailed from a family of movers and shakers. Paula Bonhoeffer's family (the von Hases), on the other hand, was a brilliant blend of sophisticated appreciation for the fine arts (on grandmother Clara von Hase's side) and for theology (grandfather Karl August von Hase was both a theologian and a son of a theologian). Dietrich's close friend and biographer Eberhard Bethge commented, "The rich world of his ancestors set the standards for Dietrich Bonhoeffer's own life. . . . He grew up in a family that believed that the essence of learning lay not in a formal education but in the deeply rooted obligation to be guardians of a great historical heritage and intellectual tradition."[2] That sense of obligation to heritage, home, family, and country—indeed, to the truth itself—would define Bonhoeffer's life.

In addition to the rich confluence of family heritage that marked his upbringing, Dietrich was born into means. The houses and summer homes the Bonhoeffers owned and occupied in and around Breslau (and later Berlin) were the perfect greenhouse environments for Karl and Paula to cultivate their rich family life. Paula homeschooled the children—intelligent and capable youngsters, all of them—who excelled in music and games and raising pets. Karl was a quiet but attentive father.

The Bonhoeffer home was exceptionally stimulating, orderly, and happy. Eric Metaxas writes, "The Bonhoeffers were that terribly rare thing: a genuinely happy family" whose "ordered life continued along through the weeks and months and years."[3]

But not particularly religious. Not that they were *irreligious*, mind you. Martin Luther's legacy still hung in the German air, a proud bit of cultural heritage. Although the Bonhoeffers did not attend church, mother Paula did make sure that her children remained connected to it and its traditions. Significant religious ceremonies were celebrated in the home and officiated by family members. The children were sent to confirmation class. Paula frequently instructed the children with stories from the Bible and encouraged them to pray, saying grace before meals and teaching them to pray privately before bed. Religious enthusiasm or emotivism of any kind was looked down on. Bethge notes, "The Christian nature of this household, then, could be sensed more under the surface or behind the scenes."[4]

THE DECISION

Thus, it came as no small surprise that the precocious, intelligent, and musically gifted Dietrich announced to the family at around fourteen that he desired to become a minister and a theologian. So outlandish did this decision seem to his siblings that they took pains to dissuade him from it. The church, they thought, was petty, boring, and feeble. Why would anyone want to give their life to such an inept institution? Undaunted, Bonhoeffer answered his siblings, "In that case I shall reform it!"[5]

What motivated this decision to give his life to theology and ministry is a matter of speculation, since Bonhoeffer himself—by nature a private person—never explained his reasons. But clearly Christ Jesus was, in these early years, beginning to woo young Dietrich to his ultimate vocation. The call of Christ to stand against the tide was at work—evidenced in his determination to press through his siblings' reproach for his chosen path. And all of this in spite of the fact that "he was not yet driven by any love of the church or an articulated theological system of beliefs, and certainly not by a discovery of the Scriptures and their exegesis."[6] Nevertheless, the Lord Jesus was calling.

Off Dietrich went to study theology at seventeen. During his student years, he had two experiences that would shape his life and theology forever. The first was a term spent studying in Rome in 1924. In Catholic Rome, Bonhoeffer witnessed something of the majesty and universality of the church of Jesus Christ for the first time, beholding an institution that transcended nation, class, and ethnicity and could stand like a bulwark against the ebb of history. The second was his encounter with the theology of Karl Barth. The novelty and freshness of Barth's approach, which emphasized the concrete revelation of God in the person of Christ through the preaching of the Word, rang true for Bonhoeffer and was the perfect complement to his experience in Rome.

Together, his study term at Rome and his exposure to Barth cemented for Bonhoeffer the notion that God—through his people, the church of Jesus Christ—is really and truly revealing, manifesting, and accomplishing his will for the world. His dissertation, *Sanctorum Communio*, centered on this very theme. There he argued that the church is a community established by God and animated by the very presence and person of Jesus, that

Christ truly dwells in the church and the church truly dwells in
Christ—not in theory but in fact. "Where the body of Christ
[the church] is," he wrote, "Christ truly is"—speaking and act-
ing, judging and saving.[7] The conclusion followed naturally:
"The church is God's new will and purpose for humanity."[8]

Whereas his family had largely overlooked and sometimes
even held the church in contempt, Bonhoeffer, by contrast,
was seeing something different, something deeper. He had both
grasped and *been grasped by* the reality that the church was the
one instrument whereby God in Christ had chosen to manifest
and extend his saving action into the world. Again, Christ was
calling.

ARRESTED BY THE CALL

This burning conviction carried him into the next years of his
life, where he threw himself both into ongoing study, expanding and deepening his convictions, and into the life of the local
church as a passionate and dedicated pastor. Through a vari-
ety of pastoral assignments, Bonhoeffer was able to put flesh
and bone to what had largely been a network of abstract and
theoretical convictions about the church. After completing his
doctorate at Berlin University, Dietrich spent a year of post-
graduate study at New York City's Union Theological Seminary.
The experience added a further layer to his theological vision.
During his time there, Bonhoeffer attended Abyssinian Baptist
Church of Harlem, an African American congregation whose
pastor preached courageously against the racism and social
injustice his parishioners faced. Bonhoeffer suddenly saw the
gospel and the church with new eyes—that in order for the

church to live up to its deepest claims about God's restorative, liberating, humanity-healing work, it must speak and act for justice, especially with and among those whose lives were threatened or marginalized by power. He would later come to express that sentiment in words repeated and remembered by his friends: "Only he who cries out for the Jews may sing Gregorian chants."[9] Once again, the radical and all-embracing call of Christ was drawing him deeper.

Thus, when he returned to Germany in 1931, Bonhoeffer found himself out of step with his environment. Invited to lecture at Berlin University and to begin his formal pastoral training, the young theologian and church leader was distressed by what he saw: a comfortable, irrelevant German church made possible by a toothless liberal theology. Bethge notes, "He now began to teach on a faculty whose theology he did not share, and to preach in a church whose self-confidence he regarded as unfounded. More aware than before, he now became part of a society that was moving toward political, social, and economic chaos."[10] Though he did not and could not know exactly what that chaos would entail, Bonhoeffer instinctively sensed that it was coming, and that both the church and the theological academy were ill-equipped to stand in its way.

At the center of Bonhoeffer's frustration with the church and the academy was the way in which both had lost touch with the radical demand of Jesus Christ, the Lord of the world and the head of the church—a demand that was increasingly laying hold of him. In fact, this period of Bonhoeffer's life represents something of a personal turning point. Though his penchant for privacy and contempt for religious sentimentality precluded his speaking openly about his inner life, it is clear by what

Bonhoeffer said and did that something profound was taking place in him. Not only did the *person* of Jesus Christ come more and more to dominate his theological vision, but the *personal call* of the Lord to Dietrich himself began to deepen. He did not call it a conversion, but a change of great magnitude was taking place in him.

Bonhoeffer's own words, written to a friend several years after the change, summarize it best:

> Then something happened, something that has
> changed and transformed my life to the present day.
> For the first time I discovered the Bible . . . I had often
> preached, I had seen a great deal of the church, spoken
> and preached about it—but I had not yet become a
> Christian. . . . I know that at that time I [had] turned
> the doctrine of Jesus Christ into something of personal
> advantage for myself . . . I pray to God that will never
> happen again. Also I had never prayed, or prayed only
> very little. . . . Then the Bible, and in particular the
> Sermon on the Mount, freed me from that. Since then
> everything has changed. . . . It was a great liberation.
> It became clear to me that the life of a servant of Jesus
> Christ must belong to the church, and step by step it
> became clearer to me how far that must go.[11]

"How far" indeed. The personal and devotional reading of Scripture, a life of prayer and concrete obedience to Jesus Christ for the sake of the church and the world—these represented the "Come, follow me" dimensions of personal faith in Christ that would ultimately lead Bonhoeffer to the gallows.

So when the Nazis rose to power in 1933, the aspiring theologian and pastor began to take his stand in gradually more bold and strategic acts of resistance. With Berlin awash in the blasphemy of the swastika, Bonhoeffer thundered,

> The church has only one altar, the altar of the Almighty
> . . . before which all creatures must kneel. . . . Whoever
> seeks something other than this must keep away; he
> cannot join us in the house of God. . . . The church has
> only one pulpit, and from that pulpit, faith in God will
> be preached, and no other faith, and no other will than
> the will of God, however well-intentioned.[12]

These bold words sprang from a heart and mind convinced that, whatever the Third Reich may have claimed for itself, the crucified and resurrected Son of God was the world's true Sovereign and Lord. Bonhoeffer's theological assault on the Reich was unrelenting. Two days after Hitler's rise, Dietrich delivered a radio address in which he criticized the entire concept of the *Führer*,[13] claiming that however much the German people might desire a national renaissance,[14] care must be taken not to make an idol out of the *Führer*. In his transcript for the address, Bonhoeffer wrote,

> The image of the Leader [*Führer*] will gradually become
> the image of the "misleader" [*Verführer*]. . . . Leaders or
> offices which set themselves up as gods mock God.[15]

Unfortunately, the radio diatribe was cut off before the final lines could be delivered. Bonhoeffer was livid, sending copies of the transcript to his friends and family so that everyone in his circle would understand both the spirit and the letter of his remarks, knowing beyond a shadow of doubt where he stood. Hitler, in Bonhoeffer's mind, was precisely the sort of *Verführer* that mocked God by his words and actions and would lead Germany inexorably to calamity if he were not stopped.

It was his theological acuity and fighting spirit that thrust Dietrich to the front of the "battle line" for the soul of Germany—and thereby put his promising pastoral and academic career on hold. With the Nazi menace breaking on Germany, no longer was it thinkable for the decisively grasped-by-Christ Bonhoeffer to entertain thoughts of a cloistered life of writing, lecturing, and pastoring. His plans would have to be reevaluated. Christ was calling him into the action, using events beyond his immediate control to shape his destiny, demanding by the challenge of each moment that Dietrich rise up as a standard of truth and clarity in the midst of a church all too ready to give way to lies, to be an advocate and defender of the weak in a nation drunk on power.

HALTING THE WHEEL

And rise he did. He believed he had no other choice. The call of Christ had come to him. Several years later, he wrote, in his classic reflection *The Cost of Discipleship*,

> Every moment and every situation challenges us to action and to obedience. We have literally no time to sit down and ask ourselves whether so-and-so is our neighbor or not. We must get into action and obey—we

TO ENTER THE UNKNOWN

must behave like a neighbor to him. . . . Perhaps you
still think you ought to think out beforehand and know
what you ought to do. To that there is only one answer.
You can only know and think about it by actually doing
it. You can only learn what obedience is by obeying. It is
no use asking questions; for it is only through obedience
that you come to learn the truth.[16]

For Bonhoeffer, the Nazi menace was no ivory-tower
abstraction for academics to debate in the friendly confines of
lecture hall or smoking room. It was an immediate and imminent threat not only to friends, family, and neighbors but also,
and most importantly, to those who would become the tar-
gets of the Reich's agenda to purge and purify German blood.
Hitler's maniacal desire to create a master Aryan race neces-
sarily included an aggressive program of eugenics—banning
interracial marriages, mandating the compulsory sterilization
of the mentally ill or deficient, euthanizing those who had been
committed to mental institutions—and ethnic cleansing, of
which the Jews were a special target. A bloodthirsty, no-holds-
barred nationalism had possessed the German soul, and many
Germans—even German *Christians*—were all too ready to cede
ground to Hitler in the name of the "greater good" (namely, the
restoration of German power and privilege).

Bonhoeffer would have none of it. As the Reich's seizure of
both the German nation and the German *church* progressed,
the question was raised as to the validity of a purely "Aryan"
church. Bonhoeffer saw right to the heart of the matter. In an
essay dating to the summer of 1933, he wrote,

What is at stake is by no means the question whether
our German members of congregations can still tolerate
church fellowship with the Jews. It is rather the task of
Christian preaching to say: here is the church, where Jew
and German stand together under the Word of God; here
is the proof whether a church is still the church or not.[17]

For Bonhoeffer, an Aryan church was simply not a church.
The very idea was blasphemy, an affront to the reconciling work
of God in Christ—a work that, according to the New Testament,
must begin in the church and move out into the world. The
lessons he had learned while worshiping at Abyssinian Baptist
Church in Harlem were clearly bearing fruit. In Dietrich's
mind, the question of the Jews was no mere ecclesiastical concern; it was not an intramural church debate. It was, instead,
an urgent question that the church—following her reconciling,
redeeming Lord—needed to put to the state. In the same essay,
Bonhoeffer contended that "the church has an unconditional
obligation towards the victims of any ordering of society, even
if they do not belong to the Christian community." And should
the state's life-destroying power continue to run riot in society,
the church would be called by her Lord "not just to bind up the
victims beneath the wheel, *but to halt the wheel itself.*"[18]

To halt the wheel itself. This was a radical and unconventional
idea. Since Luther, the German church had operated under
the notion that the church and the state occupied separate (if
complementary) spheres. Each had its own mandate from God,
and they tended to function best if they interfered with each
other as little as possible. Bonhoeffer's understanding of the
church, the world, and the universal lordship of the risen Christ

rendered this "two spheres" notion theologically and practically bankrupt. The state belonged to Jesus Christ, and the church's job was not only to remind the state of that fact but also to act against the state when and where conscience and conviction required it.

So far the call of Christ was taking Dietrich, pulling him into the vortex of a costly discipleship, quite removed from the sunny expectations of unhindered career success baked into his bourgeois Breslau upbringing. At every turn he accepted the consequences of fidelity to Christ with a characteristic blend of intelligence, creativity, and courage. When offered the pastorate of an east Berlin church in late 1933, he declined—and accepted a position in London instead. He had hoped to leverage the global ecumenical movement's strength for the sake of the "Confessing Church"—pastors, led by Bonhoeffer and Barth, who were actively resisting the Nazification of the German church. When presented with a coveted opportunity to study nonviolent resistance under Gandhi—far from the Nazi storm—he decided to head back to Germany to rejoin the fight against Hitler. When stripped of his teaching post at the University of Berlin for being an enemy of the state, he threw his energy into the work of the illegal seminaries of Zingst and Finkenwalde, equipping young pastors with the theological and practical tools they would need to build up the church in defiance of Hitler's dogmas. Whenever the concrete call of Christ came to Dietrich in the demand of the moment, he rarely, if ever, blinked.

Indeed, if ever there was a moment of hesitation, it came in June 1939 when the American theologian Reinhold Niebuhr, under whom Bonhoeffer had studied during his year of postdoctoral work at Union Seminary, came calling, offering Dietrich an opportunity to distance himself from the chaos of Germany. In New York he could teach and lecture at Union and continue with his ecumenical work. His rising star need not be snuffed out by the darkness descending on his homeland.

Bonhoeffer left for New York and immediately regretted his decision. In his heart, the well-intentioned decision was, in fact, an act of cowardice and bad faith. It was a denial of the call of Christ to him as the very person he was—a *German Christian*, son of Karl Bonhoeffer and Paula von Hase, obligated to Christ for the sake of his friends, family, heritage, and nation. He wrote to Niebuhr,

> I have made a mistake in coming to America. I must live through this difficult period of our national history with the Christian people of Germany. I will have no right to participate in the reconstruction of Christian life in Germany after the war if I do not share the trials of this time with my people. . . . Christians in Germany will face the terrible alternative of either willing the defeat of their nation in order that Christian civilization may survive, or willing the victory of their nation and thereby destroying our civilization. I know which of these alternatives I must choose; but I cannot make that choice in security.[19]

INTO THE UNKNOWN

By the end of July he was home, and the hell of total war was about to break across Europe. With the German invasion of

Poland a mere month away and the Nazis clamping down on his actions and movements, Bonhoeffer instinctively understood that the situation demanded fresh obedience to Christ. But it would also be a more uncertain and precarious kind of obedience, constituted by acts of resistance that called him out into uncharted territory. The time had come for him to leave behind the last vestige of security—as a member in good standing of the Confessing Church and an active leader in the global ecumenical movement—in order to join the Nazi military-intelligence organization known as the *Abwehr*. Working as a double agent from within the German government, Bonhoeffer was joining his strength with a far-reaching plot to overthrow Hitler's regime and lay the groundwork for a new Germany on the far side of the Reich's collapse.

Though he did not doubt the decision, it brought him no satisfaction. Bethge observes that while Bonhoeffer had made many sacrifices up to this point, joining the *Abwehr* represented a new and far deeper sacrifice: "the sacrifice of his Christian reputation."[20] What must his Confessing Church and ecumenical colleagues have thought? Bonhoeffer certainly wondered about that, as any of us would.

But hiding behind the purity of his reputation was a luxury he could, in faithfulness to Jesus Christ, no longer afford. The political, moral, and spiritual chaos of Germany represented for Bonhoeffer a "borderline situation" that suggested new duties to him—chief among which was to do all he could to aid the conspiracy to overthrow a Nazi government inebriated on innocent blood and systematically desecrating all that was good in Germany. Such a conspiracy would force Bonhoeffer to "carry camouflage and disguise to extreme limits," notes

Bethge, "so that [he] would lie better than the master liar,"[21] entrusting his everlasting destiny to the judgment and mercy of God.

Given the circumstances, such action was, in Bonhoeffer's mind, his obligation, his duty—uncertain and at times embarrassing and despicable as it must have been. In his posthumously published book *Ethics*, written from the Tegel cell he would soon find himself imprisoned in for his association with the conspiracy, Bonhoeffer wrote,

> When a man takes guilt upon himself in responsibility
> . . . he imputes this guilt to himself and to no one else; he
> answers for it; he accepts responsibility for it. . . . Before
> other men the man of free responsibility is justified by
> necessity; before himself he is acquitted by his conscience;
> but before God he hopes only for mercy.[22]

German Protestants in the wake of Luther had long believed that men and women were justified by faith in Christ Jesus alone—by casting themselves on the mercy and goodness of the God who makes himself known to us in Christ, and not by any good works. Bonhoeffer's "borderline situation" threw him into the furthest reaches of that truth. Stripped of all outer security, he had now been stripped even of the inner security that comes from knowing ahead of time that one's actions are righteous. Metaxas describes this moment as a "more demanding and more mature level of obedience" than Bonhoeffer had ever known, where a legalistic, rule-keeping approach to life that concerns itself more with personal purity than with concrete (indeed, complex) obedience had been shown to be inadequate.[23] The ambiguity of being led to this place—a place, as Jesus prophesied over Peter in John 21, he would rather not have gone—drove him into the arms of mercy like nothing else had. It was all he could hold on to. He had followed Jesus into the unknown, flinging himself into the void and trusting that he would find a gracious God there.

In April 1943, Bonhoeffer was arrested and imprisoned for his suspected association with the resistance. From his cell he reflected on the path his life had taken, the stages he had walked through in learning to yield his will and freedom to the will of God, in his poem "Stations on the Way to Freedom":

SELF-DISCIPLINE

If you set out to seek freedom, you must learn before
    all things
Mastery over sense and soul, lest your wayward desirings,
Lest your undisciplined members lead you now this way,
    now that way.
Chaste be your mind and your body, and subject to you
    and obedient,
Serving solely to seek their appointed goal and objective.
None learns the secret of freedom save only by way
    of control.

ACTION

Do and dare what is right, not swayed by the whim of
    the moment.
Bravely take hold of the real, not dallying now with what
    might be.

Not in the flight of ideas but only in action is freedom.
Make up your mind and come out into the tempest
        of living.
God's command is enough and your faith in him to
        sustain you.
Then at last freedom will welcome your spirit amid
        great rejoicing.

SUFFERING

See what a transformation! These hands so active
        and powerful
Now are tied, and alone and fainting, you see where
        your work ends.
Yet you are confident still, and gladly commit what
        is rightful
Into a stronger hand, and say that you are contented.
You were free from a moment of bliss, then you yielded
        your freedom
Into the hand of God, that he might perfect it in glory.

DEATH

Come now, highest of feasts on the way to freedom eternal,
Death, strike off the fetters, break down the walls that
        oppress us,
Our bedazzled soul and our ephemeral body,
That we may see at last the sight which here was not
        vouchsafed us.
Freedom, we sought you long in discipline, action,
        suffering.
Now as we die we see you and know you at last, face to face.[24]

Bonhoeffer had lived the path of that poem. He had left behind the world of ideas to come out into the tempest of living, guided by the command of God. Like the Lord Jesus whom he loved and followed, who in agony gave up his will to the Father in Gethsemane, Bonhoeffer had yielded his freedom into the hands of the Father. Now all that awaited him was the consummation of his costly discipleship—the final surrender of will by which he would be welcomed fully into the arms of divine Freedom itself—Father, Son, and Holy Spirit—the God who is the Life on the far side of death.

It would not be long. By April 1945, Bonhoeffer's role in the conspiracy had become known to Hitler. Enraged, he ordered that all the conspirators be destroyed. Bonhoeffer was sentenced to the gallows at the Flossenbürg concentration camp—mere weeks before Allied liberation. The camp doctor recorded later what he witnessed:

> Through the half-open door in one room of the huts I saw Pastor Bonhoeffer . . . kneeling on the floor praying fervently to his God. I was most deeply moved by the way this unusually lovable man prayed, so devout and so certain that God heard his prayer. At the place of execution, he again said a short prayer and then climbed the steps to the gallows, brave and composed. His death ensued after a few seconds. In the almost fifty years that I worked as a doctor, I have hardly ever seen a man die so entirely submissive to the will of God.[25]

He died as he had come to live: submitted to God's will.

I have loved and admired Dietrich Bonhoeffer for many years, and writing this chapter was a personal provocation for me once again to be challenged by the life of this faithful witness. Though few of us will be called into situations as extreme as brother Dietrich, the pattern of his life does, I think, provide an example for us to follow. What can we learn?

First, I think we miss the point of Bonhoeffer's life entirely if we do not understand the personal call of the risen Christ that impelled it forward. Retrospectively we can see that Jesus the Lord was at work in Bonhoeffer's childhood and student years. After his return to Berlin in the early 1930s, the call grasped him decisively and never let him go. It was his love and affection for the Lord that made his costly obedience possible.

As it is with us. Christians aren't courageous crusaders and martyrs *first*. We are ordinary folk like Peter, James, and John, like little Agnes Gonxha Bojaxhiu and precocious Dietrich Bonhoeffer, personally addressed by the Lord *first*. Everything else follows from that.

I think we *also* miss the point of Bonhoeffer's life entirely if we do not see that the personal call of the Lord to costly discipleship *took the form of* giving up his life for others. "Costly discipleship" is not heroic action considered by itself. Costly discipleship is whatever it costs us to follow the Lord Jesus in the specific ways he equips, positions, and calls us to serve our friends, families, and communities. Costly discipleship is whatever it costs us to stand with the weak, defenseless, vulnerable, and victimized. Costly discipleship is whatever it costs us to give away our lives for the good of others and the glory of God.

Sometimes, as with Bonhoeffer, that will result in dramatic acts of self-surrender. But more often, I think, costly discipleship looks like the unnoticed and unheralded martyrdom of the years—years of faithfully tending to our children, of loving our spouses and our aging parents, of serving in homeless shelters and soup kitchens, of lifting up our voices for the marginalized, of serving with our gifts in the churches and communities that Christ calls us into. These acts of faithfulness are not spectacular—but they also, in their crucified-Christ-following, self-sacrificing character, represent the blood that, as Tertullian said long ago, is the seed of the church.[26]

Finally, I think we do well to be instructed by the manner in which Bonhoeffer calmly and courageously accepted the hand that was dealt to him, without complaint and without retreat, as a faithful follower of Christ. That does not mean that he simply rolled over in passivity. Rather, at each juncture, when presented with circumstances that altered his plans, limited his options, and even, at times, challenged his mental and theological capacity, he demonstrated the kind of equipoise that comes from knowing that even in the *un*-knowing, his life was hidden with Christ in God, which made him courageous. What happened to Bonhoeffer—indeed to all of Germany—was unqualifiedly evil. And yet, God was speaking to him in it, working throughout it, summoning Dietrich into destiny.

And so it is with all of us. We are born into a world of evil. And that evil will inevitably frustrate even our noblest plans. But God is not vexed, and his good plan is not conquered by the evil we find ourselves born into. Rather, God is at work to overthrow evil from within, using its own volition against itself to bring about his Kingdom.

None of us gets out of this unscathed—that just goes with the territory. But in it all, we know that our destiny is secure and God's purpose cannot fail, and one day, *the kingdoms of this world will become the Kingdom of our Lord and of his Christ, and he will reign for ever and ever. . . .*[27]

FOR REFLECTION

"Costly discipleship is whatever it costs us to give away our lives for the good of others and the glory of God." Look at your calendar for the coming weeks. What might count as costly discipleship for you in the days ahead?

PRAYER

> *Lord Jesus Christ,*
> *Obedient Son of the Father in heaven,*
> *Thank you for the example*
> *of Dietrich Bonhoeffer's life,*
> *for the costly obedience he modeled,*
> *for the way his life still speaks.*
> *Teach me to walk with you like he did:*
> *courageous, poised,*
> *and confident in your mercy,*
> *willing to go wherever you lead me.*
> *Amen.*

THE ECSTASY, THE AGONY
Rich Mullins

*I found [Rich] such a real person, so engaging . . . incapable of being
fictitious. . . . I was stunned by the honesty, the brutal candor of his life
story. . . . I said . . . to myself, "This is what it means to live by grace."*
BRENNAN MANNING

*How do you know when God is calling you? . . . I am beginning
to recognize that . . . when God is calling, it hurts.
Maybe when God calls us, it feels like a pain.*
RICH MULLINS

And now for the final movement of our journey. We have
looked at the experience of being awakened to God the Holy
Spirit—the very Breath of God that makes us alive, in the biblical imagination, which is why the Nicene Creed declares the
Holy Spirit to be "the Lord, the Giver of Life." The Spirit bursts
forth from the innermost depths of the life of love shared by
Father and Son, breathing into our dead bodies, renewing us in
the womb of divine love, awakening us in the ecstasy of delight
that is the life of the triune God.

But the experience of the Spirit is not always ecstatic. There
are times, as we have said, that we will experience the Holy
Spirit *as* and *in* deep discomfort, for as often as the Bible speaks
of the Spirit as Wind that cools and carries us, as Breath that
enters our spiritual lungs and makes us alive, as Water that

slakes our every existential thirst, so it also speaks of the Spirit as Fire that burns us—as Karl Barth once said, "right down to faith."[1] The advent of God the Holy Spirit will unmake and remake our lives so that they are aflame with the eternal love of the triune God—the Love that he is and has; and we will experience his presence as scorching heat until we are cleansed, consumed utterly by the reality of God.

The process will hurt—in fact, it will often be agonizing—but we can rest assured that God is in it for our good. If we have eyes to see it, we will discern that he is in fact the Fire that burns with love in the many fires of our lives. When he is through, we will be radiant as God is radiant—sharers of the never-ending glory of the eternal God. That's the promise of Scripture.

While there are many great men and women who exemplify this dynamic of the spiritual life, I want to introduce you to a figure who might strike you as surprising, but whom I regard as one of the most compelling: Richard Wayne Mullins.

EARLY YEARS

If you were a fan of Christian music in the 1980s and 1990s, you likely remember where you were when you heard the news that Rich Mullins died in September 1997. I was with a group of high-school friends when we learned that Rich and his friend Mitch McVicker, who had been traveling along I-39 near Bloomington, Illinois, to Wichita, Kansas, for a benefit concert, lost control of their Jeep, flipped, and were both ejected onto the highway. When a tractor trailer swerved to avoid colliding with the overturned Jeep, it struck the badly injured Rich, who was instantly killed. He was forty-one.

With that tragic accident, Christianity suddenly lost one of its brightest flames. In the weeks that followed, people gathered all over the country to mourn the untimely death of this Spirit-saturated follower of the risen Christ. Memorial services remembered Rich and commended him into the arms of his Maker, whose face he had come to know well in the countenance of Jesus of Nazareth.

But what was it that made Rich so compelling? I believe that to answer this we must make appeal to the mysterious working of God the Holy Spirit. The book of Exodus tells us that for the construction of the Tabernacle—the movable tent of God's presence—Yahweh had chosen Bezalel son of Uri, filling him "with the Spirit of God, with wisdom, with understanding, with knowledge and with all kinds of skills—to make artistic designs for work in gold, silver and bronze, to cut and set stones, to work in wood, and to engage in all kinds of crafts."[2] The Spirit of God had anointed and filled Bezalel for the *arts*—to create a beautiful, coherent, meaning-rich space in which the presence of the utterly transcendent one could be transfigured and adored in created time. The Tabernacle would be an icon of the Presence—showing *and* mediating the life and grace of God to the people.

So it was with Rich. Not only his music but his entire life served as a brilliant, radiant icon of the presence of God. Born in eastern Indiana to John and Neva Mullins in 1955, Rich from the outset was a product of the spiritual heritage of his families of origin—in particular, his mother's. Hailing from a family of Quakers, Neva Mullins exemplified the life of tenderhearted, sensitive, compassionate holiness that would soon come to define young Rich's life. James Bryan Smith, a friend of Rich's, remarked that "Rich had a very close relationship with his mother. In her he saw many of the ideals he longed for. She was kind and nurturing . . . intelligent . . . and rarely raised her voice or spoke an unkind word."[3]

Through the steady example of Neva's life, the Spirit awakened identity in Rich, drawing him into union with the God who is all holy love. Recalling a time when she showed great kindness toward an unusual woman in their community, Rich related that through his mother's graceful witness he learned that "no one was ever won into the kingdom of God through snobbery. We come to know Christ through love."[4]

The kind of gentle love like that which he witnessed in his mother defined Rich's life. His older sister Debbie relates a time when she tried to teach Rich how to fight. He wasn't a tough kid by nature, so Debbie thought she was doing him a favor—giving Rich the tools he needed to stand up for himself on the playground. Pinned against the ground by his sister, Rich looked up and said, "Debbie, Jesus doesn't want us to fight."[5]

The Spirit of God was knitting the heart of Jesus into Rich's being. He often said that he wanted to be a missionary when he grew up, and from an early age, he showed love and concern for Native American peoples. The history of their mistreatment at the hands of white people bothered him deeply. His brother Lloyd remembers watching John Wayne movies with Rich and often seeing him cry when one of the Native Americans in the film was shot and killed. The casual, serial abuse (both in fact and in the film industry's portrayal) of these precious people wounded Rich, planting the seeds of future vocation in his soul.

THE MUSIC, THE MAN

Growing up in and around the church created the kind of environment where Rich's manifold musical gifts could begin to be realized. He began playing the piano around four years old and from the outset was, by all accounts, a virtuoso. Rich was able to play by ear. His siblings recalled that often, after they had worked tirelessly on a piece of music (without success in mastering it), Rich would sit down at the piano and play it flawlessly, even improvising it where he thought it might be improved.[6]

Music quickly became his passion, and Rich's parents recognized it. The Mullinses were not wealthy, so their dedication to his development was a great sacrifice. His father, John, a quiet, hardworking man who earned money doing manual labor and whose personality was so different from his son's, nevertheless insisted that Rich receive lessons, doing all he could to resource Rich in the flourishing of his gifts. One year, his mother went without a winter coat in order to ensure that there would be enough money to pay for his lessons, enduring the brutal Indiana winter out of love for her son.

Their sacrifices paid off. As a student at Cincinnati Bible College in the mid-1970s, Rich's Spirit-inspired talents as a singer-songwriter began to turn heads. In tandem with his band, Zion, Rich wrote prolifically, traveling as often as possible to put on concerts, in which he honed his distinctive style of salt-and-peppering nights of music and singing with sermonettes that challenged the hearts of his listeners. The ecstasy of love for God that burned in Rich's soul radiated through both what he *sang* and what he *said*.

There was something strangely magnetic about the man, his

life, and his music. To listen to his songs was to both *hear* and *experience* the realities of which he sang. His music flung the listener into the eternal made manifest in time. Dorothy Sayers, invoking Acts 2, calls this the "Pentecost of Power" that occurs when art and artist alike are working in concert with God—the dynamic energy of the art spills out beyond itself and touches those who encounter it.[7]

This was certainly the case with Rich's music—it was "Pentecostal" in the truest sense of the word. The Spirit of God who was radiant in the man was radiant also in his music. When a demo tape of Rich's songs was given to Amy Grant in the early 1980s, Grant, who was looking for material to put on a new record, was floored. "It was [the song] 'Sing Your Praise to the Lord,' . . . and it was just so interesting . . . so different. . . . By the end it reaches that crescendo, and we were all so taken by surprise. . . . It was so full of emotion."[8] Her team reached out to Rich to ask permission to record the song. He resisted at first but finally gave in. The song was an instant success, and before long, much of the Christian world in the United States was caught up in the "Pentecost of Power" that exploded from the music and lyrics of his breakout song, "Sing Your Praise to the Lord," which put Rich on the map. The years that followed saw the skyrocketing of his musical career. He wrote and recorded at a breathless pace, producing hits like "Sometimes by Step (Step by Step)," "Awesome God," "Boy Like Me/Man Like You," "Hold Me Jesus," and the way-ahead-of-its-time "Creed"—a song that puts the words of the Apostles' Creed to music, announcing in the refrain, "I believe what I believe is what makes me what I am / I did not make it, no, it is making me"—an ancient conviction that evangelicals would rediscover over the next decades.[9]

Songs like this and many more held listeners spellbound, captivated, as few before Rich have or after Rich could. His colleagues in the music world recognized the uniqueness of his gift. Michael W. Smith remarked, "There's nobody who wrote songs like Rich."[10] Rich's music not only pulsed with energy but enchanted with its originality. Gary Chapman commented that Rich "wrote such different songs. . . . They were unconventional. They were not cookie-cutter. . . . There was not one ounce of 'fat' in them. In his songs, every word needed to be there."[11] Each note, each instrument, each word served a purpose—the lyrical embodiment of the now-and-coming Kingdom of God.

Consider for a moment the breathtaking ballad "Calling Out Your Name," in which Rich describes the universe much as the ancients did—as a sacrament of the divine Presence, shot through with glory. He wrote,

Well the moon moved past Nebraska
And spilled laughter on them cold Dakota Hills
And angels danced on Jacob's stairs
Yeah, they danced on Jacob's stairs
There is this silence in the Badlands
And over Kansas the whole universe was stilled
By the whisper of a prayer
The whisper of a prayer

And a single hawk bursts into flight
And in the east the whole horizon is in flames
I feel thunder in the sky
I see the sky about to rain
And I hear the prairies calling out Your name[12]

One easily could imagine St. Francis of Assisi, whom Rich deeply admired, writing such a song eight hundred years earlier. For Rich, like St. Francis and others, there was no division between the natural world and the supernatural. The weariness that modern people feel at a universe that seems to have been explained away by the sciences was foreign to him. The natural world was mysterious and enchanting for Rich because it was enclosed within the supernatural, and God, as the Scriptures taught, was everywhere present, always gracious, working wonders. One had only to look and see in faith, and soon the face of God would make itself known everywhere, and the weary soul would be reborn in eternal freshness once again. Rich was a man soaked in wonder, ecstatic with the Spirit, ever enchanted by the glory and goodness of the God whose being transcends and encompasses the ages.

THE ANTICELEBRITY

And that was the thing about Rich: He seemed to live in another time, in another world, and by another value system. While his celebrity soared, he did not *embrace* the status that celebrity afforded him but remained humble, gentle, and servant-hearted till the day of his death. Unlike that of so many artists, Rich's music was no mirage. Rather, it surged from the center of a life that was aflame with the life-giving, love-awakening, agitating presence of God the Holy Spirit. His signature attire was old jeans and a T-shirt, and he was shoeless as often as possible. He shunned greenrooms and frequently spent the hours leading up to concerts helping workers set up chairs and get the venue ready. There wasn't a pretentious or stuffy bone in his body, for the Spirit had illuminated Rich with the unpretentious love of the mendicant God, Jesus, and he reflected it wherever he went.

As one who, by the Spirit, had been drawn into deep friendship with Jesus, Rich was deeply concerned about the seduction of fame. So while fame often sought him, he did not seek it. Rich's sister related a time when he was playing at Radio City Music Hall. He said to her, "The one thing that I have found more seductive than anything is applause. . . . I'm going to have to watch that. . . . You can't imagine what it feels like to have . . . a thousand people . . . applauding you . . . that approval. . . . I could really get lost in that."[13]

Thus he fought tooth and nail against the siren song of fame. Refusing to be anything other than what his Creator had made him to be, Rich struck those who met him as the genuine article—an utterly authentic human being. The Catholic priest and author Brennan Manning said of the first time he met Rich, "I found him such a real person, so engaging. . . . I said to myself, 'This guy is incapable of being fictitious.' I was stunned by the honesty, the brutal candor of his life story. . . . Rich laid bare his whole life with Jesus, and I said . . . to myself, 'This is what it means to live by grace rather than by performance.'"[14] At a time when the plague of Christian celebrity was beginning to take hold in the United States, Rich was the anticelebrity.

Indeed, for Rich, as it was with fame, so it was with money. Unlike so many who see money in more or less neutral terms, Rich understood that money (as Jesus taught) had the power to act as a rival god, competing for allegiance, cutting kindness at the root, planting hell in the person who gave way to its deceptions. Rich refused to be undone by the spiritual power of money, and he took concrete steps to avoid it, famously setting a board of overseers to watch over the income he made from his albums and tours. According to Rich's wishes, the board paid him what the average workingman in America made that year. The rest was given away.

As a result, during his career, Rich never personally saw more than around $24,000 of his total income in a given year. At one point, one of his producers asked him how much money he earned per quarter. Rich had no idea. He remarked, "If I knew how much it was, it'd be so much harder to give it away."[15]

While his humble Indiana upbringing combined with his Quaker roots certainly had much to do with Rich's thirst for a life of simplicity and generosity, the real source went deeper. The Spirit had awakened in Rich an understanding of the person of Christ Jesus and the requirements of the gospel—and it was this that really fueled his convictions about money. James Bryan Smith notes, "Because Rich saw money as a distraction from the kingdom . . . he believed that if God made you rich He was not doing you a favor. Possessing wealth presented a great challenge to the believer, Rich thought; quite often discipleship meant enduring suffering, giving away one's treasures, and sacrificing for the good of others."[16]

It was that sense of the radicality of the gospel that made Rich so unusual on yet another front: his understanding of Jesus' heart for the poor and oppressed. Years before much of the evangelical world would rediscover the Bible's dream for social and economic justice, Rich Mullins was busy becoming mesmerized with the great St. Francis of Assisi, who, many centuries earlier, had abandoned all worldly possessions to live a life of simple obedience to Jesus, preaching the gospel, serving the poor, healing the sick, and working for peace, justice, and reconciliation wherever he went.

St. Francis's radical, Spirit-fueled obedience to the call of Jesus inspired Rich. "I just became fascinated," he said, "with the character of Saint Francis. What I saw . . . was a man who had fallen in love with God, someone for whom God is everything. And that was one of those things that propelled me. I started reading about Francis and the Franciscan movement and asking the question, 'What would it be like if we took the gospel that seriously?'"[17]

The Spirit of divine love that burned in St. Francis was burning now in Rich with the same kind of intensity, challenging not only the shape and structure of his own life but that of his listeners as well. At a concert he related,

> And this is what I've come to think: that if I want to
> identify fully with Jesus Christ, who I claim to be my
> Savior and Lord, the best way that I can do that is to
> identify with the poor. This I know will go against
> the teachings of all the popular evangelical preachers,
> but they're just wrong. They're not bad, they're just
> wrong. Christianity is not about building an absolutely
> secure little niche in the world where you can live with
> your perfect little wife and your perfect little children
> in a beautiful little house where you have no gays
> or minority groups anywhere near you. Christianity

is about learning to love like Jesus loved, and Jesus loved the poor, and Jesus loved the broken.[18]

It was that conviction that compelled Rich to leave Nashville for Wichita, Kansas, where he would attend Friends University, working to complete his degree in music education so that he could teach children on a Navajo Indian reservation, bringing to fruition a love for Native American peoples that the Spirit had planted in him when he was young. This he eventually did, leaving Kansas to live in a hogan on a reservation located in Tse Bonito, New Mexico. When asked once about the reason for the move, Rich stated bluntly, "The truth is . . . I just kind of got tired of a white, evangelical, middle-class sort of perspective on God, and I thought maybe I would have more luck finding Christ among the pagan Navajos."[19]

Rich knew that Christ loved and had promised to be present to those whom society pushed to the side, and he determined to find him there. Till the day of his death, Rich lived with a handful of his friends among the precious Navajo people, teaching music, sharing life with them. He loved them. And they loved him. And their life together was a powerful embodiment of the love that the triune God is and has—indeed, the love that God intends all creation to one day share.

In Tse Bonito, that love was made manifest, and it, along with Rich's entire and highly unusual way of being, served as a provocation to those who took notice of it. No wonder that at the Dove Awards a year after he died, Amy Grant, in tribute to Rich, called him "the uneasy conscience of Christian music."[20] His ecstatic love for God and passionate commitment to the historical person of Jesus Christ made it impossible for

Rich to accept the status quo—either in his own life or in the world around him.

SOMETIMES WHEN GOD CALLS, IT HURTS

But no account of Rich's life would be complete if it did not speak of the agony that he knew so well. The apostle Paul—no stranger to inner anguish—once put it like this:

> We know that the whole creation has been groaning
> as in the pains of childbirth right up to the present
> time. Not only so, but we ourselves, who have
> the firstfruits of the Spirit, groan inwardly as
> we wait eagerly for our adoption to sonship,
> the redemption of our bodies.[21]

Paul understood that we live in an anguished world that groans for its final redemption. Believer and unbeliever alike are bound up in the agony of the present time. And in fact, Paul seems to think that being touched by the Spirit, who is the firstfruits of the great redemption yet to come, does not *lessen* our anguish but in fact *heightens* it. As a starving man's pangs of hunger are not lessened but heightened by the first taste of food, so the believer's anguished appetite for deliverance is not satiated by the Spirit but made—dare we say it—worse. When the promise of redemption is held up against the distress of our present world, when the first morsel of manna from the heavenly city touches our lips, the agony is all the greater.

And yet, Paul insists we understand that it is with respect

to this very hope of redemption that we are saved. As we learn to lean into the agony, we become suffering-yet-hopeful, anguished-yet-joyful, groaning-yet-grateful witnesses to the love of God in Christ.[22]

For all of his creativity, spontaneity, and playful innocence, Rich was well acquainted with the groan. His relationship with his father, John, who neither understood nor fully appreciated him, left deep marks on Rich's psyche. John was a stern, cold, demanding, and often angry father whose children strove to please him, and Rich most of all, with little success.[23] Despite his support of Rich's musical gifts, John struggled to make sense of his son, once remarking that he had two sons, two daughters, and a piano player.[24] The father-wound haunted Rich his entire life, creating a thirst for redemption that came through in so much of his music and ministry.

Additionally, so would the feeling of being generally unloved, misunderstood, and out of place. Born in Hoosier country and raised among practical, hardworking Midwestern farmers and tradespeople, the highly sensitive, artistic, and musically gifted Rich stood out like a sore thumb. Nonathletic and nonmechanical to the core, Rich spent his childhood feeling like a misfit, remarking later in life, "When I was young, I was angry . . . [saying to God], 'God, why am I such a freak? . . . Why couldn't I be just like a regular guy?'"[25] The agony of not knowing his place would remain with Rich till the day he died.

Furthermore, friends and family remark that there was something of the prophet's way of seeing the world in him from an early age. And as for many of the prophets of old, it caused him deep discomfort. He could sense people's pain; he was uniquely attuned to injustice; he was cut to the quick by the reality of a world that did not function as God desired— all marks of a prophetic soul. And, like many prophets, he felt odd for it. His sister Debbie commented, "When he was in high school he was thinking about things that . . . normal high-school kids just don't think about. . . . It was in a good way that he wasn't normal, but I also know that he felt a lot of loneliness because of it, because he felt separate from most normal people, and he recognized his difference. . . . I think it probably had to be pretty frustrating to him at times."[26]

While the ache to find an enduring sense of place dogged Rich, he also, over time, learned to access it in creative ways that brought life to others. His friends at Cincinnati Bible College described him as someone who was "aloof . . . [and] bizarre,"[27] who wrote "hopelessly, oppressively dark" songs that would dramatically resolve out of insights God had given him from Scripture.[28] From the deep wells of his own ache, Rich was learning how to draw forth a beauty that would bless the world. James Bryan Smith remarks that Rich "would work out his pain, as well as his highest aspirations, through music"[29] as songs like "Hold Me Jesus," "Bound to Come Some Trouble," and "Verge of a Miracle" bear witness to.

But it wasn't only through his music that Rich would work out his pain; it was also through his unique gifts at building community—the spiritual agony gave rise to an ecstasy, a "going out" toward others that drew people into friendship. One friend noted that "every single place he went, he created community." His thirst for a people and a place to call home throughout his life flowered into a kind of social magnetism; and yet, for all that, the communities he created were places that "he never felt completely a part of."[30] Another friend related, "Rich always had either an individual or a group that he would confide himself in, but rarely was it everything. And if he did confide everything, then he would remove himself. . . . Rich wrestled with a number of different issues and wrestled with them his whole life. To me it goes back to that idea of, 'Do you really accept me? . . . Do you really love me if you know how dark I really can be?'"[31]

He was well acquainted with the darkness—not only the darkness of loneliness and an enduring sense of isolation but the darkness of hardship, loss, and disappointment. Rich endured the loss of family members, the difficulty and confusion stemming from a broken engagement, and the disappointment of finding not only Nashville but also, later, his move to the reservation in New Mexico not being what he thought they would be. The agony, for Rich, in greater and lesser degrees, was ever present—and often unrelenting.

Yet, as time went on, he began to see that in the hands of God, the fires of agony could be a source of light and blessing for others. In a playful yet serious-minded essay for *Release* magazine in the summer of 1994, Rich crafted a brilliant analogy for the life of faith, comparing the human situation to that of a fiddle in the hands of an expert fiddler:

> Now, although a fiddle may never be fooled by the folly of human thinking, very much like us, they have pain. Their necks are stiff and their nerves, their strings, are stretched. They feel the friction of the bow, and inside their beautiful brown little bodies they have only a little stick called a sound-post and an emptiness that seizes

every inch of space—top to bottom, side to side. Their emptiness is for them (as it is for us) a nearly unbearable ache—an ache that is fitted to the shape that makes its tone. And sometimes a fiddle is tempted to fill that void with rags or glass or gold, even knowing that, if it should do that, it would never again resonate the intentions of its fiddler. It would never again be alive with his music. It would dull itself to the exquisite heat of the fiddler's will, the deliberate tenderness of his fingers.[32]

Because the fiddle can only resonate with the fiddler's music by maintaining the delicate balance of friction, tension, and—above all—emptiness, Rich understood that the fiddle must not try to fill itself with anything other than the gracious will of the fiddler. It must, in a sense, *befriend* its own agony, emptiness, and desolation, offering it up daily to the creative genius of the fiddler. So it was, Rich thought, with the human life: It must be empty in order to be filled with the life-giving music of the Spirit. Gradually, Rich embraced the ancient counsel of befriending (as St. Francis had) Lady Poverty and finding the embrace to be a source of strength, virtue, and wisdom, touching the sacred Fire that burned in the fires of inner agony, and being purified in the process. He commented,

How do you know when God is calling you? Well . . . in my own life, I think that for years I tried to avoid loneliness, because it hurts to feel lonely. Now I'm beginning to recognize that maybe that's what it feels like when God calls me. Maybe when God is calling, it hurts. Maybe when God calls us, it feels like a pain.

. . . For years in my own life, I tried to drown that pain,
I tried to avoid that pain, I tried to fill that ache with . . .
a lot of stuff that was destroying me. . . . To listen to the
call of God means to accept some of the emptiness that
we have in our own lives, and rather than always trying
to drown out that feeling of emptiness, . . . [we] allow
that to be a door through which we go to meet God. . . .
And this is where I think moral purity begins to play in.
. . . Almost everything that corrupts us is something that
we use to fill some kind of ache, some kind of emptiness.
. . . Moral purity might be nothing more than a call to
accept the ache and to accept the emptiness, and to allow
ourselves to go through that to where God is calling
us to go.[33]

It was insights like this one—forged in the fires of personal,
existential anguish—that made Rich Mullins the spiritually
vibrant, authentically human figure that he was. And though
he was not perfect—none of us are—what marked him was
his refusal to do anything less than submit to the Spirit's burning, purifying work—the work that makes us, finally, like Jesus
Christ, eternally obedient Son of the eternally delighted Father
in heaven. Brennan Manning put it best:

Jesus of Nazareth ruined Rich Mullins's life. And out
of the ruins He recreated a ragamuffin of startling
originality; no human being who has crossed my path
even remotely resembles him.[34]

The Spirit had burned Rich right down to Jesus.

When I first outlined this book, I did not intend to conclude it with a chapter on Rich Mullins. Truth be told, he was the furthest thing from my mind. I had originally planned on writing on Teresa, Bonhoeffer, and perhaps St. Francis of Assisi. But, I thought, in keeping with Teresa and Bonhoeffer, wouldn't it be better to pick a more contemporary figure?

One sunny Saturday morning, a friend of mine, David Burchfield, sat on the porch with me, drinking coffee and listening to me describe my quandary. He thought about it for a minute and then quipped, "What about Rich Mullins?" After a bit of conversation followed by an afternoon's worth of research, I knew I had my guy.

Rich Mullins to me exemplifies what it means to live a life given over to the ecstasy and agony of engagement with God the Holy Spirit. And he does that in three ways.

First, Rich's life reminds us that God the Holy Spirit is the one who awakens us to divine love, and the extent to which we live in love is the extent to which we are filled with the Spirit. Rich loved the God made known in Jesus passionately, because he knew that the God made known in Jesus loved *him* passionately. Love had awakened love in him and kept on awakening it and deepening it, with the result that as Rich's life unfolded, so also did the love of God in the world. Not only his songs but the entire manner of his life bore witness to what the apostle Paul called "the love of God that is in Christ Jesus our Lord."[35]

Second, Rich's life reminds us that to the extent the Spirit draws us into the ecstatic love of God, this experience will also, as often as not, put us at odds with the world around us. The Spirit, as we have learned, draws us into Christ Jesus, which means that we will have—at the very least—an awkward relationship with the entire value system of the world. The Spirit will conform us to the person of Jesus Christ, making us humble, giving us a great love for the poor and dispossessed, and we will therefore find ourselves at times the glad resisters of the seductions of this age as we bear happy witness to the life of the age to come. Though the shape of our resistance will differ from Rich's (as our circumstances differ), resist we will, for we can do no other, as the Spirit keeps hiding our lives ever deeper with Christ in God.[36]

Third, Rich's life is a powerful reminder that the experience of the Spirit is not just ecstasy but agony as well. He is the Fire that burns behind the many fires of our lives—not only the ones *around* us but the ones *inside* us as well. I have been a pastor for many years now, and there is not a single person I have met who does not live with some kind of agony: the pain of loss, deferred hope, unmet expectation, traumas that haunt even while we seek healing. All of these can become, if we will let them, doorways to holiness, places of encounter with God, bushes that burn but don't burn up, through which the living God meets with us and speaks with us to make us as he is:

All flame.

FOR REFLECTION

Where in your everyday life do you find yourself "at odds with the world around us" as a consequence of your relationship with the triune God? What gives you comfort and courage in those experiences?

PRAYER

Spirit of the Living God,
Thank you for the
example of Rich Mullins's life:
for the way in which
he made manifest
the love that the
triune God is and has.
Fill me also with that love,
that my life,
in both ecstasy and agony,
may be a vibrant witness
of the life
of the age to come.
Amen.

EPILOGUE

Christian spirituality means living in the mature wholeness
of the gospel. It means taking all the elements of your life—
children, spouse, job, weather, possessions, relationships—
and experiencing them as an act of faith.

EUGENE PETERSON, *The Contemplative Pastor*

In the spring of 2014, I began working on a project with a few of my pastor friends—a multichurch effort to explore the connections between Christian faith and human labor. While we were still in "dream phase," one of them said, "What if we flew out to Montana to interview Eugene Peterson?" Best known as the author of *The Message* translation of the Bible and widely regarded as something of a modern church father, Eugene—who then was in his early eighties—had spent his entire pastoral career helping people understand how their lives, in their totality, were arenas for the glory of God to be revealed. In one way or another, all of his thirty-plus books addressed the topic. *Who better,* we thought, *to talk to us about it than Eugene?*

As it turns out, one of my close friends, Daniel Grothe,

knew Eugene well and was able to arrange a visit. Moreover, the group decided that I would be the one to interview Eugene.

I was giddy with delight.

Eugene had become a personal hero of mine when I first read his book *A Long Obedience in the Same Direction* during my seminary years. His hero status was further cemented when I began ministry at our church plant in Denver and was desperate for wise guides who could help me understand my work. Books like *Working the Angles, Practice Resurrection, Under the Unpredictable Plant,* and *The Pastor* helped me make sense of what I was supposed to be doing, and as a consequence, in one way or another, Eugene's sagely presence had been with me every day of my first five years as a pastor in that community. To meet "The Pastor" himself would be the privilege of a lifetime.

It also, in full disclosure, made me fantastically nervous. *What if this goes horribly wrong? What if I get so starstruck that I can't utter a coherent sentence? What if he gets frustrated with me and bails out on the interview? How will I ever live the humiliation down?* I was a bit of a wreck.

My tensions, as it turns out, were eased the moment we walked through Eugene and Jan's door. There we met the warm aura of nonpretentious, easy hospitality. They hugged us—even though three out of our group's four were complete strangers—welcomed us into their home, made us comfortable, and began asking us questions—about our families and our ministries, what we were working on, and so forth.

Eugene in particular sat and listened to us with a rapt and relaxed attention. He was all there, totally present, and curious. I remember thinking, *You're Eugene Peterson. You're a big deal. Like, a* huge *deal. And yet, you keep treating us like we're actually interesting. Like we have something to say. Like we* matter. He honored us by his entire manner of being.

When interview time rolled around, he carried that same relaxed, attentive presence with him. As I asked him my questions, I kept finding myself listening less to *what* he was saying in response and more to *how* he was saying it. The way he received each question, taking a deep breath—sometimes several—weighing my words against what he had learned over the years, and then finally, and only after what felt like an eternity, giving his careful and considered response. His presence. His regard. His depth. It all left such a profound impression on me.

But there was more. In and around all of that, I will never forget the glint in his eyes and the way that every now and again, a smile would break across his face like lightning illuminating the dark sky on a stormy summer night, an echo of Uncreated Light's glad announcement "Let there be light," which had once exploded at the dawn of the universe.

There is a name for what we experienced during those two days with Eugene. The name for it is *holiness*. And as I have said all along in this book, it is not the privileged possession of a select few. It is, rather, the design of God for every human life. Yielding to the work of the Spirit who makes us like Jesus, we will live up to the invitation of Israel's God who says, "Be holy as I am holy."[1]

It is easy, I think, to complain that others have it easier in this regard than we do. We look at people like Eugene Peterson,

Mother Teresa, Dietrich Bonhoeffer, and Rich Mullins, and think, *But surely the conditions of their lives were more favorable to holiness than mine.*

You must put that out of your mind—and the sooner, the better. No one's life is more optimized for holiness than another's. We are fashioned from the same clay by the same Hands, breathed into by the same Breath, summoned by the same Son in whose image and likeness we are made. And in each of our lives, in all their unrepeatable uniqueness, it is the same triune God who calls us, speaking to us in our circumstances, wooing us to glory.

Will we respond? All we could ever want or desire—an eternal and happy union with God, our Final Good—is on the table for us. We just need to say yes. And keep saying yes.

By conviction and experience, I know that these things are true, for that same warmth of holiness I witnessed in Eugene I have also witnessed in the lives of countless other men and women of faith in my life. I have seen it in doctors and lawyers, in baristas and schoolteachers, in hard-charging businessmen and businesswomen, in grandmas and grandpas, and in stay-at-home moms and dads.

I have also, here and there, seen it in professional "religious" types—pastors and worship leaders, preachers and theologians—but (believe me when I say this) the preponderance of holiness among the professionally religious is not higher than that among those who live more (so-called) normal lives. In fact, I think I often find more holiness in the pew than on the platform, and this, I believe, is what keeps the church going—that there are men and women courageous enough to stay in it with the triune God, through ups and downs and highs and lows, through seasons of spiritual plenty and through some-times dreadfully long seasons of gnawing desolation. They stay in it because they are drawn by the beauty that is God. Where else would they go?

God is present to you, friend. Your background, your limi-tations, your circumstances, even your failures—none of it, in the end, really matters. For in all things and at all times, *it is God with whom you deal*—Father, Son, and Holy Spirit, mold-ing you into the divine image, filling you with his splendor, illuminating your life with his glory, and so bringing blessing and healing to the world.

Do you believe that?

I hope that you do, for if you will, you—even you—can become "all flame."

ACKNOWLEDGMENTS

Every book (like every human endeavor) grows out of the soil of relationship and is nurtured in community. That's a rather round-about way of saying: I have a lot of people to thank.

To my beloved bride of twenty years, Mandi: I realize that as I've grown older, I've also grown more eccentric. I am genuinely sorry for that. Sort of. Thank you for loving me in my eccentricity, tirelessly supporting this project, and keeping our family's life together robust and sane and sound. I love you with my whole heart.

To my kids, Ethan, Gabe, Bella, and Liam: Being your dad is an outrageous privilege. I've loved every second of it. Thank you for being who you are. Keep it up. Also, who's up for s'mores tonight?

To my parents, Bill and Nancy: The quality of holiness I talk about on these pages I first witnessed in you. I couldn't have asked for better parents, and I thank God daily for you.

To my siblings, John, Anna, and Rob: The longer I live, the more I realize how lucky I am that we get to call each other family. You're a gift.

To my publisher, Don Pape: The biggest unexpected blessing of this whole process has been the honor of being able to call you not just my publisher but my dear friend. Mandi and I got much more than we bargained for when the Lord partnered us with you. We are so grateful.

To my editors, Dave Zimmerman and Elizabeth Schroll: You made this a much better book than it would have been otherwise. Plus, you're fun to work with. Thank you for your efforts on this project.

To my agent, Alex Field: I laugh when I think about the conversation at Starbucks that gave rise to this project. *"I've never done this before, but what if . . ."* So you said, and so it began. I'm humbled and grateful for your belief in me and in my writing, and I'm deeply honored to be working with you. Let's keep it up.

To my pastor, Brady Boyd: Thanks for taking on a guy who came in limping and more than a little bewildered. You've created a space at New Life for me and my family to heal and flourish in ways we never thought possible. We love you and are so thankful for you.

To my brothers, Daniel Grothe, Glenn Packiam, Jason Jackson, Brad Baker, Jon Egan, Jeremiah Parks, and Brett Davis: Being able to count you all as friends makes me a wildly rich man.

To my dear friend David Blankenship: "You met me at a strange time" is one way to describe our relationship. Another is this: "A friend loves at all times, and a brother is born for adversity" (Proverbs 17:17, RSV). You've been both: a friend at all times and a brother in deep adversity. Mandi and I love you and Janie, and we are so grateful for your friendship.

To the good people of New Life Church: You're the family we didn't know we needed till we arrived here. We owe you a debt of gratitude we could never repay. Thank you for receiving us with your warm, generous, open hearts. We're going to keep doing our best for you.

To my dear friends at Bloom Church: No community has taught me more about finding God in the hard places than you. Being able to serve as your pastor for seven years was the honor of a lifetime. It still makes me emotional to think about. You drew things out of me I didn't know were in me; indeed, many of the most central ideas of this book first took shape in sermons and conversations with you. I found my voice with you and will always cherish our time together. Thanks for letting me be your pastor.

And finally, to the saints of Believers Church, Marshfield, Wisconsin, circa 1981–1999: "There were giants . . . in those days" (Genesis 6:4, NKJV). The example of your lives has been with me every single day of my ministry. I hope that how I live honors you.

QUESTIONS FOR DISCUSSION

INTRODUCTION

1. What has the spiritual journey been like for you?

2. What has been most surprising to you about your walk with God so far?

3. What has been most challenging?

4. What resonates most with you about the picture of the spiritual life presented here in the introduction?

5. Describe someone you've encountered on your journey whose life most reflects the character of God. What most stands out to you about them?

6. If you had to describe the "moment" you are in spiritually, what words would you use?

7. What are you most excited about learning from this book?

CHAPTER 1: AWAKENING TO THE FATHER

1. What about the image of God as "Father" resonates with you? Why?

2. What, if anything, about the image of God as "Father" makes you uncomfortable?

3. How does reimagining God's fatherhood through Jesus' person and experience change that image?

4. Describe an experience you have had of the love of God. What was it like? What, if any, changes in your life came about as a result of it?

5. Who is someone in your life who seems to have embraced the reality of God as "Father"? What about that person's faith stands out to you?

6. Take a minute to reread the quote from Karl Barth near the end of the chapter. Do Barth's words comfort you? Challenge you? How?

7. Where do you need to experience God's fathering love in Christ more?

CHAPTER 2: FOLLOWING JESUS, THE LORD

1. What does "following Jesus" mean to you?

2. How has this chapter challenged or broadened your understanding?

3. When did you first begin to follow Jesus? What has changed in your life as a result?

4. Describe a time in your life when the call of Jesus took you somewhere you did not expect.

5. Do you agree or disagree that we need to hear the message and invitation of Jesus afresh? Why or why not?

6. What is something you've felt Jesus calling you to lately?

7. Are there places where you sense Jesus calling you out of safety and comfort? What is holding you back?

CHAPTER 3: FILLED WITH THE SPIRIT

1. What is your "default" image of the person and role of the Holy Spirit?

2. How has this chapter challenged and deepened that image?

3. Having read this chapter, reflect on an experience you've had of the Holy Spirit. What kinds of words would you use to describe it?

4. What was your reaction to the connection between the Spirit and resurrection? How does that challenge your understanding of the Holy Spirit?

5. What are some areas where you need to open your life more fully to the Holy Spirit?

6. How would your devotional life change if you began to incorporate focused time welcoming and waiting on the Holy Spirit?

CHAPTER 4: THE PURIFYING FIRE

1. Have you ever heard the Holy Spirit described as "Fire" before? How does this chapter's presentation of the Spirit compare with what you have heard in the past?

2. What was your reaction to the idea that the Spirit is often experienced as agony?

3. Have you ever experienced the Holy Spirit as, as this chapter said, "the Fire that burns in the fires of [y]our agony"? If so, how did God shape your character in and through that experience?

4. Why do you think the presentation of the Spirit as Fire in this chapter is sometimes difficult for people to recognize and accept?

5. What are some places in your life right now that the Lord may want to touch with the purifying fire of his Spirit?

6. What would change if you began to recognize the Spirit as the Fire that burns in, with, and under the many little fires that burn in your life?

CHAPTER 5: THE STORY WE DIDN'T EXPECT

1. Describe a time that your life took a turn you didn't expect.

2. How did you experience that time spiritually? What did the Lord do in you through it?

3. How did this chapter's discussion of the will challenge or deepen your understanding of the goal and purpose of human freedom?

4. How did this chapter challenge and enrich your interpretation of the spiritual value of seasons where the story takes a turn you didn't expect?

5. What was your reaction to this chapter's presentation of the idea of Providence? How does that compare or contrast with your own understanding?

6. Are there places in your life now where, rather than fighting, you need to enter into the gift and grace of self-abandonment? What are they?

7. What would it look like for you to embrace Henri Nouwen's presentation of Christian maturity (page 118)?

CHAPTER 6: THE HIDDEN FACE

1. When in your life have you experienced spiritual darkness? What was it like?

2. What strategies do you usually use to cope with that darkness?

3. What was your reaction to the idea of the value of darkness when reading this chapter?

4. Describe the difference between "sensing" God and "perceiving" God as described in this chapter.

5. How might what was taught in this chapter change the way you think about times of aridity, darkness, and inward desolation?

6. How might it change the way you experience those times?

7. How might it change the way you walk with others through those times?

CHAPTER 7: TO OFFER GOD THE EMPTINESS

1. What, if anything, did you know of Mother Teresa's experience of inner darkness before reading this chapter?

2. What was something that surprised you about Teresa's inner darkness?

3. What do you make of Teresa's eventual understanding of her inner darkness? Does that understanding resonate with you? Why or why not?

4. Explain in your own words how Teresa's spiritual experience increased her compassion for others. Why is that important for understanding our own experiences of darkness?

5. What did you notice about how Teresa handled her experience of inner darkness with spiritual directors, friends, and pastors?

6. How might that be helpful to you or others?

CHAPTER 8: TO ENTER THE UNKNOWN

1. What, if anything, did you know of Dietrich Bonhoeffer's life before reading this chapter?

2. What was something that surprised you about Bonhoeffer's life?

3. What do you make of how the call of Christ gradually unfolded in Bonhoeffer's life, eventually gripping him at the deepest possible level?

4. What about Bonhoeffer's experience of the call resonates with you?

5. Explain in your own words how Bonhoeffer's understanding of the call of Christ increased his determination to resist the evil of his day. Why is that important for our own understanding of the call of Christ?

6. What did you notice about how Bonhoeffer faced his death?

7. How can Bonhoeffer's life inform your own obedience to the call of Christ?

CHAPTER 9: THE ECSTASY, THE AGONY

1. What, if anything, did you know about Rich Mullins before reading this chapter?

2. What was something that stood out to you about Rich's life?

3. What are some of the evidences in Rich's life that he was full of the Holy Spirit?

4. What did you think about the way in which Rich's saturation in the Spirit put him at odds with things like money, success, and fame? What can we learn from that?

5. Explain in your own words how the Spirit used some of the inner "agonies" that Rich lived with to bless the world.

6. What did you make of Rich's analogy between the fiddle and the human situation?

7. How might your life, in the same way, become a "fiddle" fit for the Great Musician to play?

NOTES

INTRODUCTION

1. Romans 8:19.
2. Haran is also called Paddan Aram; see Genesis 28:2.
3. Genesis 28:12-15.
4. In Christian theology, these two things—God the exalted, transcendent, sovereign one, and God the everywhere-present "with you" one—are actually two ways of talking about the same thing. One way of understanding it is that God is so otherly other than us (transcendent) that he is not bound or limited in any way by created space or time—which means that he is present to all things at once (everywhere present) as their very source. Neat, right? Paul put it best: "In him we live and move and have our being" (Acts 17:28).
5. Genesis 28:16.
6. Genesis 28:17.
7. Genesis 4:1, RSV.
8. Genesis 32:24-30.
9. 2 Corinthians 3:18.
10. Benedicta Ward, *The Sayings of the Desert Fathers* (Kalamazoo, MI: Cistercian Publications, 1975), 103. An "office" was a form prayer that many of the ancients used, and many people still use today, as a help to prayer.
11. Psalms 18:19; 31:8.

1: AWAKENING TO THE FATHER

1. Emphasis added. Here's the full text of the Apostles' Creed. I recite it often in my devotional times. It helps remind me of the story we're all living in, and who it is that governs and guides that story: "I believe in God, the Father Almighty, Creator of heaven and earth. I believe in Jesus Christ, his only Son, our Lord, who was conceived by the Holy Spirit, born of the Virgin Mary, suffered under Pontius Pilate, was crucified, died, and was buried; he descended to the dead. On the third day he rose again; he ascended into heaven, is seated at the right hand of the Father, and will come again to judge the living and the dead. I believe in the Holy Spirit, the holy catholic [universal] church, the

communion of saints, the forgiveness of sins, the resurrection of the body, and the life everlasting. Amen."

2. Luke 11:1.

3. John 1:18.

4. Luke 9:18 (emphasis added).

5. Luke 11:2-4.

6. The Lord's Prayer, based on Matthew 6:9-13, parallels and expands on the prayer from Luke 11 and includes the traditional "For thine is the Kingdom . . ." closing line.

7. Luke 2:47.

8. Luke 2:48 (emphasis added).

9. Luke 2:48-50 (emphasis added).

10. Deuteronomy 1:31.

11. Isaiah 63:16.

12. Jeremiah 31:9.

13. Exodus 3:15.

14. With the exception of his cry of abandonment on the cross—which we will get to in a later chapter.

15. Matthew 3:17.

16. John 8:29.

17. Acts 17:28.

18. Augustine expounds the *vestigia trinitatis* at length in the second half of *De Trinitate*.

19. Matthew 7:11.

20. Henri J. M. Nouwen, *The Return of the Prodigal Son: A Story of Homecoming* (New York: Image Books, 1992), 49.

21. Colossians 1:19-20, MSG.

22. Karl Barth, *Church Dogmatics*, ed. G. W. Bromiley and T. F. Torrance, vol. 4, *The Doctrine of Reconciliation*, part 1 (Edinburgh: T&T Clark, 1961), 157.

23. See Philippians 2:7.

24. Barth, *Church Dogmatics* vol. 4 part 1, 158–159. One of the things you see over and over again in Christian theology is that because God as triune is never divided against himself, the action of one member of the Trinity is always understood as involving the others. This is a good example of that. For Barth, when *God the Son* goes into the far country for us, *God the Father* and *God the Holy Spirit* are also involved in the action. This insight will be important throughout this book.

25. John 17:25-26.

2: FOLLOWING JESUS, THE LORD

1. Priscilla Meyer, in an introduction to Fyodor Dostoevsky, *Crime and Punishment* (New York: Barnes & Noble Classics, 2007), xviii.

2. As told in Priscilla Meyer's introduction to Dostoevsky, *Crime and Punishment,* xviii.

3. Flannery O'Connor, in an essay entitled "Some Aspects of the Grotesque in Southern Fiction" (1960). See http://www.en.utexas.edu/Classes/Bremen /e316k/316kprivate/scans/grotesque.html.

4. Dallas Willard, *The Divine Conspiracy: Rediscovering Our Hidden Life in God* (San Francisco: HarperSanFrancisco, 1998), 11 (emphasis added).

5. Matthew 4:18-22.

6. Matthew 9:9.

7. Matthew 4:17.

8. Compare to John's preaching in Matthew 3:2. The message is exactly the same.

9. Wolfhart Pannenberg, *Jesus—God and Man,* 2nd ed., trans. Lewis L. Wilkins and Duane A. Priebe (Philadelphia: Westminster Press, 1977), 61.

10. John 1:22-23.

11. See Pannenberg, *Jesus—God and Man,* 61.

12. Psalm 24:1. The divine name Yahweh is translated into English as "Lord."

13. Zechariah 14:9.

14. Psalm 110:1.

15. Acts 2:36.

16. Matthew 1:21.

17. Luke 24:36-43.

18. I am quoting from Pannenberg, *Jesus—God and Man,* 283. Pannenberg, a twentieth-century German theologian, grasped this truth as well as anyone.

19. Romans 10:9-10.

20. Larry W. Hurtado, *Why on Earth Did Anyone Become a Christian in the First Three Centuries?* (Milwaukee, WI: Marquette University Press, 2016), 132 (emphasis added).

21. Philippians 3:7-11.

22. See Romans 1:5; 16:26.

23. J. R. R. Tolkien, *The Fellowship of the Ring* (New York: Ballantine Books, 1973), 81–82.

3: FILLED WITH THE SPIRIT

1. I should state for the record here that I *do* still believe in miraculous healings, signs and wonders, and gifts of the Holy Spirit—all the "fantastical" stuff. I love it all. This chapter won't be about that, however. What I want to try to do here is spell out the basic, baseline experience of the Spirit.

2. John 20:17.

3. John 20:18.

4. John 20:19-22.

5. Acts 1:4-5.

6. Genesis 1:1-3.

7. As stated in the Nicene Creed.

8. Isaiah 55:11, ASV.
9. St. Ambrose, *On the Holy Spirit*, quoted in Thomas C. Oden, *Systematic Theology* vol. 3, *Life in the Spirit* (San Francisco: HarperSanFrancisco, 1994), 36.
10. St. Basil the Great, *On the Holy Spirit*, trans. Stephen M. Hildebrand (Crestwood, NY: St. Vladimir's Seminary Press, 2011), 53.
11. Robert W. Jenson, *Systematic Theology* vol. 1, *The Triune God* (New York: Oxford University Press, 1997), 86.
12. Isn't it neat how those metaphors work together?
13. Psalm 104:27-30.
14. The "[and the Son]" was a later addition to the fourth-century Niceno-Constantinopolitan Creed, which resulted in a great deal of controversy that continues to this day. Many Christians feel comfortable with the addition on the grounds that it helps us remember that the Spirit's reality has everything to do with the shared life and love of the Father and the Son, as we will later see.
15. Ezekiel 37:5-6.
16. Ezekiel 37:10.
17. Romans 8:11.
18. 1 Peter 3:18.
19. Hebrews 6:4-5.
20. 1 Corinthians 12:3.
21. Romans 8:15.
22. St. Augustine, *Confessions* book 1 (Uhrichsville, OH: Barbour, 2013).
23. St. Augustine, *Confessions* (New York: Penguin, 1961), 231–32.
24. Galatians 5:22-23.
25. Acts 2:38-39.
26. 1 Thessalonians 5:17, NKJV.
27. Acts 2:2.
28. John 3:34.

4: THE PURIFYING FIRE

1. Benedicta Ward, *The Sayings of the Desert Fathers* (Kalamazoo, MI: Cistercian Publications, 1975), 103.
2. Luke 3:7-9.
3. Psalm 50:3.
4. Psalm 50:2.
5. Genesis 15:17.
6. Exodus 3:2.
7. Exodus 13:21.
8. Deuteronomy 4:24.
9. Luke 3:16.
10. 2 Timothy 2:21.
11. 1 Peter 1:6-7.

12. St. Teresa of Avila, *The Interior Castle* (New York: Dover, 2007), 74.
13. St. Gregory of Nyssa, *On the Soul and the Resurrection*, trans. Catharine P. Roth (Crestwood, NY: St. Vladimir's Seminary Press, 2002), 83.
14. St. Gregory of Nyssa, *On the Soul*, 84.
15. C. S. Lewis, *The Problem of Pain* (San Francisco: HarperOne, 2001), 39–40.
16. Lewis, *Problem of Pain*, 91 (emphasis added).
17. Acts 17:28.
18. Genesis 50:20 (emphasis added).
19. Jeanne Guyon, *Experiencing the Depths of Jesus Christ*, Library of Spiritual Classics vol. 2 (Sargent, GA: SeedSowers, 1975), 35.
20. John O'Donohue, *Anam Čara* (New York: HarperCollins, 1998), 6.
21. Thomas Merton, *New Seeds of Contemplation* (New York: New Directions, 2007), 257.
22. Merton, *New Seeds*, 258.
23. Merton, *New Seeds*, 14–15.

5: THE STORY WE DIDN'T EXPECT

1. Luke 22:39-42.
2. Luke 22:44.
3. Mark 14:36 (emphasis added).
4. John 19:30.
5. Jeff Myers, "The Corrupting Power of Sin," Summit Ministries, January 18, 2013, summit.org/resources/articles/the-corrupting-power-of-sin/.
6. William Ernest Henley, "Invictus" (1875).
7. Genesis 1:28.
8. Genesis 2:16.
9. Genesis 2:17.
10. John 8:34.
11. John 8:36.
12. John 12:25.
13. Romans 6:3-4.
14. Hans Urs von Balthasar, *Prayer*, trans. Graham Harrison (San Francisco: Ignatius, 1986), 60.
15. Judson W. Van DeVenter, "I Surrender All" (1896).
16. Matthew 16:17-19.
17. Matthew 16:21.
18. Matthew 16:22.
19. Matthew 16:23.
20. Matthew 16:24-27.
21. George MacDonald, "The Creation in Christ," *Unspoken Sermons* series 3 (public domain), http://www.gutenberg.org/cache/epub/9057/pg9057-images.html.
22. From the hymn "Christos Anesti."

23. Song of Songs 5:16.
24. Helen Howarth Lemmel, "Turn Your Eyes upon Jesus" (1922).
25. Luke 1:38 (my paraphrase).
26. Henri J. M. Nouwen, *In the Name of Jesus: Reflections on Christian Leadership* (New York: Crossroad, 1989), 81.
27. Hebrews 12:2.

6 THE HIDDEN FACE

1. Psalm 27:4-10.
2. Numbers 6:24-27 (emphasis added).
3. 1 Timothy 6:16.
4. Acts 17:28.
5. Exodus 33:20-23.
6. 1 John 4:8.
7. This would obviously be a misapplication of Paul's words in 2 Corinthians 3:18, CEB.
8. C. S. Lewis, *The Screwtape Letters* (New York: HarperOne, 2001), 38 (emphasis added).
9. Lewis, *Screwtape Letters*, 37–38.
10. Lewis, *Screwtape Letters*, 38–39. Remember this is a demon speaking here. References to "He" and "His" and the "Enemy" are references to God. Likewise, when Screwtape mentions "Our Father Below," he is, of course, referring to the devil.
11. Lewis, *Screwtape Letters*, 39–40.
12. Richard J. Foster, *Prayer: Finding the Heart's True Home* (San Francisco: HarperSanFrancisco, 1992), 17.
13. *The Cloud of Unknowing, with the Book of Privy Counsel*, trans. Carmen Acevedo Butcher (Boston: Shambhala, 2009), 22.
14. St. Francis de Sales, *Consoling Thoughts on Trials of an Interior Life*, comp. Père Huguet (Charlotte, NC: TAN Books, 2013), 57.
15. St. Francis de Sales, *Consoling Thoughts*, 58, 61 (emphasis added).
16. St. John of the Cross, *Dark Night of the Soul*, trans. E. Allison Peers (Mineola, NY: Dover, 2003), 19.
17. John Frederick Nims, trans., *The Poems of St. John of the Cross*, 3rd ed. (Chicago: University of Chicago Press, 1979), 19, 21.
18. Isaiah 50:10.
19. Genesis 15:12.
20. Psalm 97:2.
21. Job 9:11.
22. Psalm 88:18.
23. 2 Corinthians 5:7.
24. Mark 15:34.
25. Psalm 139:7-12.

26. James 1:17.
27. Galatians 5:22-23.

7: TO OFFER GOD THE EMPTINESS

1. Kathryn Spink, *Mother Teresa: A Complete Authorized Biography*, rev. ed. (New York: HarperOne, 2011), 4.
2. Spink, *Mother Teresa*, 6.
3. Spink, *Mother Teresa*, 6.
4. Spink, *Mother Teresa*, 8.
5. Spink, *Mother Teresa*, 17.
6. Paul Murray, *I Loved Jesus in the Night: Teresa of Calcutta—A Secret Revealed* (London: Darton, Longman and Todd, 2008), 38.
7. Teresa, in a private letter to the Archbishop of Calcutta, September 1959. As quoted in Brian Kolodiejchuk, *Mother Teresa: Come Be My Light; The Private Writings of the "Saint of Calcutta"* (New York: Doubleday, 2007), 39–40.
8. As quoted in Kolodiejchuk, *Mother Teresa: Come Be My Light*, 341.
9. Brian Kolodiejchuk, *Where There Is Love, There Is God: Mother Teresa* (New York: Doubleday, 2010), 27.
10. Spink, *Mother Teresa*, 55.
11. "Mother Teresa (1910–1997)," Biography.com, last updated February 24, 2020, biography.com/religious-figure/mother-teresa.
12. Kolodiejchuk, *Mother Teresa: Come Be My Light*, 44.
13. A postulator in the Catholic church is the person responsible for guiding the process of beatification and canonization.
14. Kolodiejchuk, *Mother Teresa: Come Be My Light*, 133–34.
15. Kolodiejchuk, *Mother Teresa: Come Be My Light*, 149.
16. Kolodiejchuk, *Mother Teresa: Come Be My Light*, 154.
17. Kolodiejchuk, *Mother Teresa: Come Be My Light*, 154.
18. Kolodiejchuk, *Mother Teresa: Come Be My Light*, 163.
19. Kolodiejchuk, *Mother Teresa: Come Be My Light*, 180.
20. Kolodiejchuk, *Mother Teresa: Come Be My Light*, 214.
21. Murray, *I Loved Jesus*, 68 (emphasis added).
22. Spink, *Mother Teresa*, 301–302.
23. Murray, *I Loved Jesus*, 69.
24. Father Michael van der Peet, as cited in Kolodiejchuk, *Mother Teresa: Come Be My Light*, 269.
25. Kolodiejchuk, *Mother Teresa: Come Be My Light*, 326.
26. Psalm 139:7.

8: TO ENTER THE UNKNOWN

1. Dietrich Bonhoeffer, *The Cost of Discipleship* (New York: Touchstone, 1995), 89. So famous, in fact, that Chris Tomlin and Matt Redman made it into a popular worship song, "The Wonderful Cross."

2. Eberhard Bethge, *Dietrich Bonhoeffer: A Biography* (Minneapolis, MN: Fortress Press, 2000), 13.

3. Eric Metaxas, *Bonhoeffer: Pastor, Martyr, Prophet, Spy* (Nashville: Thomas Nelson, 2010), 25.

4. Bethge, *Dietrich Bonhoeffer*, 36.

5. Bethge, *Dietrich Bonhoeffer*, 36.

6. Bethge, *Dietrich Bonhoeffer*, 44.

7. Dietrich Bonhoeffer, *Sanctorum Communio: A Theological Study of the Sociology of the Church* (Minneapolis, MN: Fortress Press, 2009), 140.

8. Bonhoeffer, *Sanctorum Communio*, 141.

9. It is not clear where, if ever, this was written, but Bonhoeffer's friends attributed this maxim to him. Biographer Eric Metaxas places it around the time of the passing of the Nuremberg Laws in 1935 (*Bonhoeffer*, 281); others place it earlier (or later).

10. Bethge, *Dietrich Bonhoeffer*, 173.

11. Bethge, *Dietrich Bonhoeffer*, 205.

12. Bethge, *Dietrich Bonhoeffer*, 257.

13. *Führer* simply means "leader," and this title Hitler would ultimately take to himself in the sense of a "supreme leader," answerable to no one.

14. The aftermath of World War I was a source of deep bitterness for many German people. The Treaty of Versailles, which brought WWI to an end, imposed territorial, financial, political, and military penalties and restrictions upon Germany and was felt by most of her citizenry to be overly harsh, vindictive, and finally, unfair. That bitterness was a key factor in laying the groundwork for the rise of the charismatic Adolf Hitler, who promised to bring about a return of German pride and prestige.

15. Bethge, *Dietrich Bonhoeffer*, 260.

16. Bonhoeffer, *Cost of Discipleship*, 78.

17. Bethge, *Dietrich Bonhoeffer*, 273.

18. Bethge, *Dietrich Bonhoeffer*, 274–75 (emphasis added).

19. Bethge, *Dietrich Bonhoeffer*, 655.

20. Bethge, *Dietrich Bonhoeffer*, 678.

21. Bethge, *Dietrich Bonhoeffer*, 794.

22. Dietrich Bonhoeffer, *Ethics* (New York: Touchstone, 1995), 244.

23. Metaxas, *Bonhoeffer*, 367.

24. Dietrich Bonhoeffer, "Stations on the Way to Freedom" (translated by Neville Horton Smith), as recorded in Bonhoeffer, *Ethics*, 19.

25. Bethge, *Dietrich Bonhoeffer*, 927–28.

26. Tertullian, *The Apology* (Pickerington, OH: Beloved, 2015), 83. Tertullian worded it this way: "The oftener we are mown down by you, the more in number we grow; the blood of Christians is seed."

27. Revelation 11:15 (my paraphrase).

9 THE ECSTASY, THE AGONY

1. Karl Barth, *Church Dogmatics*, eds. G. W. Bromiley and T. F. Torrance, vol. 2, *The Doctrine of God*, part 2 (New York: T&T Clark, 2010), 205.
2. Exodus 31:3-5.
3. James Bryan Smith, *Rich Mullins: An Arrow Pointing to Heaven* (Nashville: B&H, 2000), 13.
4. Smith, *Rich Mullins*, 13.
5. Debbie Mullins, *Rich Mullins: A Ragamuffin's Legacy*, directed by David Schultz (2014; Chandler, AZ: Bridgestone Multimedia Group, 2016), DVD, approx. 6:00.
6. Sharon Roberts, *Rich Mullins: A Ragamuffin's Legacy*, approx. 8:00.
7. Dorothy L. Sayers, *The Mind of the Maker* (San Francisco: HarperSanFrancisco, 1987), 112.
8. Amy Grant, *Rich Mullins: A Ragamuffin's Legacy*, approx. 32:00.
9. The ancient formula *lex orandi, lex credendi* summarizes it nicely—what we pray (and sing!) is what we believe, and it shapes how we live. In the late 1990s, through the influence of folks like the late Robert Webber, evangelicals began to rediscover this, leading to the renaissance of liturgy we are currently seeing in historically low-church, evangelical Christianity. In retrospect, it is remarkable to think about how Rich anticipated this.
10. Michael W. Smith, *Rich Mullins: A Ragamuffin's Legacy*, approx. 41:00.
11. Smith, *Rich Mullins*, 120.
12. Rich Mullins, "Calling Out Your Name," *The World as Best as I Remember It*, vol. 1 (Brentwood, TN: Reunion Records, 1991).
13. Debbie Mullins, *Rich Mullins: A Ragamuffin's Legacy*, approx. 1:02:00.
14. Brennan Manning, *Rich Mullins: A Ragamuffin's Legacy*, approx. 1:03:30.
15. Reed Arvin, *Homeless Man: The Restless Heart of Rich Mullins*, directed by Ben Pearson (Myrrh Records and Compassion International, 1998), approx. 15:30.
16. Smith, *Rich Mullins*, 154.
17. Smith, *Rich Mullins*, 166.
18. Rich Mullins, *Rich Mullins: A Ragamuffin's Legacy*, approx. 56:00.
19. "Rich Mullins Interview—Ichthus Festival, 1996," YouTube video, 11:28, posted by "Ragamuffin Archive," last accessed April 13, 2020, youtube.com /watch?v=7zQOX8NmC0c, approx. 0:50.
20. "1998—Rich Mullins Tribute," YouTube video, posted by "GMA Dove Awards," January 29, 2014, youtube.com/watch?v=NNra3f8Hsl0, approx. 6:01.
21. Romans 8:22-23.
22. See Romans 8:24-39.
23. Moon Mullins, "God, Dad, Me, and Rich Mullins: A Few Thoughts on Rejection," *MoonsThoughts* (blog), May 2, 2014, moonsthoughts.com /richmullins-post/.

24. Edwin L. Carpenter, review of *Rich Mullins: A Ragamuffin's Legacy*, directed by David Leo Schultz, Dove.org, accessed January 22, 2020, dove.org/review/12136-rich-mullins-a-ragamuffins-legacy/.

25. Smith, *Rich Mullins*, 25.

26. Debbie Mullins, *Rich Mullins: A Ragamuffin's Legacy*, approx. 15:00.

27. Gary Rowe, *Rich Mullins: A Ragamuffin's Legacy*, approx. 18:30.

28. Elizabeth Lutz, *Rich Mullins: A Ragamuffin's Legacy*, approx. 19:30.

29. Smith, *Rich Mullins*, 21.

30. Sharon Roberts, *Rich Mullins: A Ragamuffin's Legacy*, approx. 24:30.

31. Gary Rowe, *Rich Mullins: A Ragamuffin's Legacy*, approx. 25:00.

32. Rich Mullins, *The World as I Remember It: Through the Eyes of a Ragamuffin* (New York: Multnomah, 2004), 74–75.

33. Rich Mullins, *Rich Mullins: A Ragamuffin's Legacy*, approx. 2:00:00.

34. Brennan Manning, foreword to Smith, *Rich Mullins: An Arrow Pointing to Heaven*, x.

35. Romans 8:39.

36. See Colossians 3:3.

EPILOGUE

1. Leviticus 19:2 (my paraphrase). See also Leviticus 21:8; 22:32; John 17:11.

THE NAVIGATORS® STORY

T HANK YOU for picking up this NavPress book! I hope it has
been a blessing to you.

NavPress is a ministry of The Navigators. The Navigators began
in the 1930s, when a young California lumberyard worker named
Dawson Trotman was impacted by basic discipleship principles and
felt called to teach those principles to others. He saw this mission as
an echo of 2 Timothy 2:2: "And the things you have heard me say in
the presence of many witnesses entrust to reliable people who will
also be qualified to teach others" (NIV).

In 1933, Trotman and his friends began discipling members of the
US Navy. By the end of World War II, thousands of men on ships and
bases around the world were learning the principles of spiritual multi-
plication by the intentional, person-to-person teaching of God's Word.

After World War II, The Navigators expanded its relational ministry
to include college campuses; local churches; the Glen Eyrie Conference
Center and Eagle Lake Camps in Colorado Springs, Colorado; and neighborhood and citywide initiatives across the country and around the world.

Today, with more than 2,600 US staff members—and local ministries in more than 100 countries—The Navigators continues the transformational process of making disciples who make more disciples, advancing the Kingdom of God in a world that desperately needs the hope and salvation of Jesus Christ and the encouragement to grow deeper in relationship with Him.

NAVPRESS was created in 1975 to advance the calling of The Navigators by bringing biblically rooted and culturally relevant products to people who want to know and love Christ more deeply. In January 2014, NavPress entered an alliance with Tyndale House Publishers to strengthen and better position our rich content for the future. Through *THE MESSAGE* Bible and other resources, NavPress seeks to bring positive spiritual movement to people's lives.

If you're interested in learning more or becoming involved with The Navigators, go to www.navigators.org. For more discipleship content from The Navigators and NavPress authors, visit www.thedisciplemaker.org. May God bless you in your walk with Him!

Sincerely,

DON PAPE
VP/PUBLISHER, NAVPRESS